The Complete Wok Cookbook

200 Easy and Flavorful Home-Made Chinese Recipes for Beginners and Advanced Users to Master Stir-Frying, Steaming and Dim Sum

Dalian Lee

Copyright© 2022 By Dalian Lee All rights reserved.

No part of this book may be reproduced, transmitted, or distributed in any form or by any means without permission in writing from the publisher except in the case of brief quotations embodied in critical articles or reviews.

Legal & Disclaimer

The content and information in this book is consistent and truthful, and it has been provided for informational, educational and business purposes only.

The content and information contained in this book has been compiled from reliable sources, which are accurate based on the knowledge, belief, expertise and information of the Author. The author cannot be held liable for any omissions and/or errors.

Once you use the information and contents contained in this book, you have automatically agreed to hold harmless the Author from and against any costs, damages, and expenses, including any legal fees potentially resulting from the application of any of the information provided by this book.

Content

Introduction 1

Chapter 1 The Tradition of Wok Cooking 2

History of Wok Cookery 2
Benefits of Using a Wok 2

Chapter 2 Wok Kitchen 4

Selecting a Good Wok 4
Setting up a Wok-Friendly Pantry with Supplies .. 5
Seasoning and Cleaning 5
Conclusion 6

Chapter 3 Vegetables and Sides 8

Stir-Fried Bean Sprouts with Carrot 8
Suzhou Five Spice Bok Choy with Cashews 11
Bok Choy with Ginger 8
Ningbo Stir Fry Vegetables 11
Grape Chutney with Herbes 8
Tasty Vegetarian Tanzanian Skillet 11
Garlic Eggplant 8
Stir-Fried Garlic Spinach 12
Mediterranean Baby Bok Choy 9
Honey Brussels Sprouts 12
Simple Cambodia Corn 9
Basic Stir-Fried Cabbage 12
Asian Teriyaki Cauliflower and Kale 9
Teriyaki Vegan Combo 12
Curry Veggie Caribbean Style 9
Garlic Broccoli 12
Chinese North Bok Choy 10
Vegetarian Bok Choy 13
Asian Wok Sticky Tofu and Veggies 10
Broccoli with Braised Mushrooms 13
Tianjin Stir Fry Vegetables 10
Healthy Baby Romaine with Goji Berries 13
Asian Wok Veggies with Peanut Butter Sauce .. 10
Brussels Sprouts with Pistachios 13
Stir-Fried Bok Choy 11
Maple Brussels Sprouts Stir Fry 14
Luncheon Brussels Sprouts with Broccoli 11
Simple Stir-Fried Tomato and Eggs 14

Chapter 4 Beans and Legume 16

Authentic Beans Caprese 16
Green Bean with Chicken Thighs 17
Ginger Orange Lentil Stew 16
Venetian Garlic Beans 18
Seared Tofu with Green Beans and Coconut Sauce
.... 16
Noodles with Green Beans and Cabbage 18
Caramelized Balsamic Bean with Onion 18
Saucy Green Beans Skillet 17
Mexican Wok Black Beans and Zucchinis 18
Asian Yellow Peas with Spinach 17
Curry Garbanzo with Tomato 19

Quinoa Fried Rice with Beans ....19 Healthy Black Beans with Apples 19

Chapter 5 Grain and Rice 21

Spam Pineapple Fried Rice.............................21
Indian Fried Rice with Onion 21
Japanese Fried Rice with Bacon 21
Couscous Ghardaïa with Mushroom 22
Alexandria Nutty Rice Casserole.....................22
Steamed Rice with Chinese Sausage and Bok Choy
....22
Basmati Rice with Cashews 23
Mixed Nut Pilaf with Herbes 23

Shrimp Fried Rice with Peas 23
Indonesian Tomato Egg Fried Rice 23
Chinese Sausage Fried Rice with Peas 24
Fried Rice with Smoked Trout 24
Fried Rice with Shrimp and Egg......................24
Simple Sinangag 25
Kimchi Fried Rice with Mushroom 25
Vegetable Egg Fried Rice................................25

Chapter 6 Pasta 27

Honey Chow Mein with Vegetable.......................27
Cold Scallion Noodles 27
Fried Vermicelli Noodles with Mushrooms...........27
Rice Noodles with Beef and Broccoli..................28
Singapore Noodles with Shrimp 28
Asian Spicy Pasta with Tomatoes....................29
Hakka Noodles with Pork and Cabbage..............29
Chinese Birthday Noodles with Shrimp 29

Tasty Beef Chow Fun 30
Sesame Noodles with Peanut Butter................30
Seafood Lo Mein with Pork...............................30
Beef Lo Mein with Bean Sprouts 31
Egg Noodles with Scallions 31
Chicken Chow Mein with Bok Choy................32
Canton Pancit..32

Chapter 7 Fish and Seafood 34

Curried Shrimp with Basmati 34
Fried Chips and Cod Fish...............................34
Ginger Mussels in Black Bean Sauce 34
Shrimp and Pork with Lobster Sauce 35
Pan-Fried White Fish with Soy Sauce 35
Thai White Fish and Vegetables......................35
Sweet Vietnamese Scallops and Cucumbers......36
Asian Stir-Fried Chili Clams...............................36
Spicy Shrimp with Pineapple and Papaya...........36
Light Seafood Congee....................................37
Quick Shrimp with Lobster Sauce 37

Bay Scallops with Snow Peas 37
Simple Ginger and Scallion Crab 38
Teriyaki Salmon with Sugar Snap....................38
Chinese Steamed Fish 38
Korean Spicy Stir-Fry Squid 39
Japanese Miso Cod with Tea Rice 39
Stir-Fry Shrimp and Broccoli...............................39
French Inspired Halibut 40
Sichuan Mussels and Shrimp 40
Malaysian Chili Squid and Celery....................40
Easy Salt and Pepper Shrimp 40

Mussels with Tomato Sauce 41
Salmon and Vegetables with Oyster Sauce 41
Garlic King Crab with Hoisin Sauce....................41

Chapter 8 Salads 43

Seafood Salad 43
Savory Bean and Tomato Salad 43
Simple Myriam's Salad 43
Peppery Bean and Spinach Salad.....................43
Turkey and Bean Salad 44
Tuna and Beans Salad 44
Butternut Squash and Bean Salad 44
South American Pasta and Beef Salad 45
Steak with Arugula Salad...................................45
Roasted Red Pepper and Edamame Salad 45

Chapter 9 Soups and Stews 47

Simple Sweet Peanut Soup................................47
Stir-Fried Bok Choy, Egg and Tofu Soup............47
Pork and Shrimp Wonton Soup 47
Chinese Chicken Stock 48
Chinese Mushroom and Carrot Soup 48
Tomato and Egg Drop Soup 48
Ginger Egg Drop Soup 48
Hot and Sour Noodle with Pork Soup 49
Healthy Pork Congee 49
Sizzling Rice and Shrimp Soup 49
Hot and Sour Beef and Carrot Soup..................50
Hot-Sour Seafood and Vegetables Soup...........50
Healthy Pork and Egg Drop Soup 50
Chicken and Walnut Pomegranate Stew...........51
Chicken and Vegetables Stir-Fry Soup..............51

Chapter 10 Poultry 53

Mexican Stir Fry Chicken and Black Beans........53
East-Indian Chicken with Apricot Preserves.......53
Pad Thai Chicken and Rice Noodles..................53
Sesame Honey Chicken 54
Chicken with Chipotle Gravy 54
Cheesy Chipotle Chicken Sandwich..................54
Honey Chicken 55
Classic General Tso's Chicken 55
Chicken with Asparagus 55
Coconut Chicken Thigh 56
Ginger Chicken in Peanut Oil 56
Orange Chicken and Sugar Snap......................56
Stir-Fried Chicken and Mushroom.....................57
Cilantro-Lime Chicken and Pineapple 57
Sweet and Sour Pineapple and Chicken............57
Lemongrass Chicken and Bok Choy 58
West African Chicken and Tomato Rice 58
Chicken with Bamboo Shoots and Mushrooms...58
Sesame Oil Ginger Chicken 59
Chicken and Bacon Rice 59
Chicken Stir Fry with Peanut Butter...................59
Kadai Chicken with Yogurt.................................59
Malay Whole Chicken Curry 60
Garlic Chicken with Cashew Nuts 60
Yellow Curry Chicken with Cauliflower 60
Curry Chicken, Carrot and Zucchini 60
Chicken with Walnuts 61
Garlic Kimchi Chicken and Cabbage.................61

Cambodian Chicken Basil Pesto 61
Chicken and Vegetables with Hoisin Sauce 61
Orange Chicken with Sesame Seeds 62

Chapter 11 Pork, Beef and Lamb 64

Mexican Mac n Cheese with Beef 64
Hoisin Pork and Snow Peas Stir-Fry 64
Pork with Bok Choy and Carrot 64
Beef Empanadas 65
Quick Peking-Style Pork Ribs 65
Stir-Fried Pork Ribs with Black Bean Sauce 65
Beef and Butternut Squash Stir Fry 66
Italian Sausage Pot Pie 66
Stir-Fried Ginger Lamb 66
Easy Quesadillas 67
Lamb Leg with Ginger and Leeks 67
Sichuan Cumin-Spiced Lamb 67
Lamb with Pear and Prunes 68
Pork Ribs with Black Bean Sauce 68
Beef Tenderloin with Shiitake Mushrooms 68
Mongolian Beef Steak 69
Beef with Honey and Oyster Sauce 69
Beef Steak and Bell Peppers Stir-Fry 69
Honey Pork 70
Steamed Egg with Ground Pork 70
Sichuan Twice-Cooked Pork with Leek 70
Beef Ramen with Pepperoni Stir-Fry 71
Sichuan Beef with Carrot 71
Twice-Cooked Pork Belly with Black Bean Sauce
.... 71
Andouille and Basmati Rice 72
Sesame Carrots and Steak Stir Fry 72
Orange Sesame Beef 72
Corned Beef 73
Beef with Cranberry Sauce 73
Sweet and Sour Beef Stir Fry 73

Chapter 12 Snacks and Desserts 75

Shrimp and Water Chestnuts Dumplings 75
Pork and Mushroom Lettuce Wraps 75
Japanese Cumin Chicken Stir Fry 76
Shrimp with Roasted Peanuts 76
Egg Foo Yong with Peas 76
Vanilla Banana Bites 77
Easy Tomato Egg Stir-Fry 77
Crab Egg Foo Young Patties 77
Appetizer Bok Choy 78
Spice Popcorn 78
Honey Shrimp with Walnut 78
Honey-Garlic Chicken and Broccoli 79
Chicken and Black Beans Tacos 79
Quick Drunken Shrimp 79
Hoisin Sesame Tofu 80
Five-Spice Pork Meatballs 80
Steamed Cabbage and Carrot Dumplings 80

Appendix 1: Measurement Conversion Chart 81

Appendix 2: Recipes Index 82

Introduction

Now you can cook restaurant-style authentic Chinese food right in your kitchen using the right ingredients and a good Wok. I never knew the importance of a Wok until I started using it myself. Making stir fries, dim sims, noodles, soups, and stews then became super easy. The fact that a wok disperses heat much more evenly than a conventional frying pan is one great benefit of it. This is caused by the Wok's concave design, which has sloping sides, as well as the material used to make it. Less hot or cold areas result from improved heat distribution, which guarantees that all of the food in the Wok is cooked through at the same time. That is why the taste and texture of the food cooked in a Wok have no parallel. And if you want to try the same, then the Wok recipe collection from this cookbook will definitely help you. But first, let's learn a little more about Wok cooking and how it is worth trying!

Chapter 1 The Tradition of Wok Cooking

A Wok is recognized as a cooking pot having a spherical bottom and high sides, typically with two side handles or one bigger handle. Food cooks faster in a Wok because heat is dispersed more evenly than in a saucepan due to the Wok's rounded bottom. When cooking a stir fry, for example, the high sides make it easier to toss stuff into the pan, allowing the components to mix and cook evenly.

History of Wok Cookery

Over 2000 years ago, during the Han dynasty, the Wok was thought to have been created for the first time in China. Early versions of the Wok, which is Cantonese for "cooking pot," were created of cast iron metals, which made them more enduring and sturdy. In the Canton province of China, where fuel was scarce, this hybrid of a saucepan and a frying pan was first developed. Typically, there was only one fireplace in a house, so the entire dinner had to be prepared on it. The Wok was hung directly over the fire to make the greatest use of the limited fuel. Its design and the substance used to create it made it a good conductor of the heat released by the flickering flames beneath it. Before cooking, all of the components were coarsely diced, cutting down on cooking time and using less expensive wood. Nowadays, a wide variety of foods are prepared in the Wok all over the world. The majority of Woks are made of carbon steel, which enables them to be lightweight to pick up while yet being strong and nonstick.

Benefits of Using a Wok

The Wok is indispensable when preparing Asian cuisine, it has a wide range of applications. One of the world's most adaptable cooking utensils, the Wok may be used for a variety of cooking methods, including:

- Stir-frying
- Steaming
- Pan-frying
- Deep frying
- Boiling
- Braising
- Searing
- Smoking
- Stewing

Because of the design, heat can be transmitted evenly throughout the entire Wok, ensuring that all of your components are cooked at the same time. Moreover, a huge advantage of using a Wok is that you can cook with very little oil and yet have delicious, nonstick food. You may occasionally need additional items for your Wok, such as a Wok lid for steaming or boiling food or even a Wok ring to prevent your Wok from sliding around while cooking.

Quick Cooking

While Woks can be used for a variety of cooking activities, stir-frying, a speedy and wholesome method of food preparation, is the most popular usage for them. Thanks to the inventive design of Woks, which effectively distributes the tremendous heat around the pan, food cooks quickly and evenly. The food made with the stir-fry technique gets a rich flavor.

Multipurpose

Although stir-frying may be the main purpose of Woks, they are actually far more versatile in the kinds of food that can be prepared. These cooking techniques include steaming, poaching, deep-frying, braising, boiling, searing, stewing, and smoking food. They do almost all of the tasks that a traditional frying pan would, frequently better.

Healthy Food

Wok cookery is an easy and great way to make healthy food. This is due to the fact that stir-fried meals are frequently prepared with fresh, healthy ingredients, the high heat uses less oil than traditional frying, and the short cooking procedure preserves the food's nutritional value.

One Pan Cooking

A Wok would be the only pan I would bring if I were stranded on a desert island. The ability to use a single Wok to cook multiple meals is the major reason behind that. They take less storage space. In a single wok you cook different types of ingredients together and they all taste great.

Cooks Bulk Food

The higher usable volume of Woks is one aspect that makes them superior to conventional frying pans for cooking. You can cook considerably more food in a Wok than in a frying pan because of its form and higher edges. Cooking for more people is possible, as is preparing more food at once to store for later.

Simple Preparation

A stir-fry is easy, fast, and simple to make when you have a wok in your kitchen. In order to ensure even cooking, you select your fresh ingredients and cut them all into bite-sized pieces. Then you add the ingredients after heating the oil in the Wok. Although some Wok dishes can be more difficult, stir-fries are normally quick and easy to prepare.

Retain Its Original Texture

Due to the Wok cooking, the dish retains a lot of its texture and doesn't get oily or soggy. While meats and seafood don't absorb a lot of fat, vegetables maintain their snap and crispness.

No Expensive Equipment Needed

When you are cooking in a wok, you don't need expensive tools to make a single meal. You can use:

- A wooden spoon or another object to stir the pan.
- A scraper to remove every bit of food.
- Anything soft to scrub the Wok.

It's mainly an inexpensive way to cook, though additional items like a serving spoon and a Wok lid can be added.

Long Lasting

Woks are made out of materials that long lasting and as they are used over time they tend to get a coating layer over the surface which keeps the Wok protected.

Chapter 2 Wok Kitchen

To cook good Chinese food at home, you will need suitable essentials and supplies in your kitchen. And to help you set up the perfect Wok kitchen, let me discuss some of the things that I learned while using a Wok for cooking.

Selecting a Good Wok

You know the saying, "You get what you pay for?" One of the uncommon situations where it does not apply is this one. A good carbon steel Wok lasts forever. It transfers heat evenly and is also reasonably priced. Asian chefs with experience recommend carbon steel Woks above the many other types available today, including those made of aluminum, stainless steel, and even copper.

Is the Bottom Flat or Round?

Use of a flat-bottom Wok is recommended if you are using a Western electric range burner. Round-bottomed Woks may reflect heat, damaging the element. A flat-bottomed Wok can be used with gas burners.

Handle with Care

Woks were designed to be easily lifted into and out of the conventional Chinese wood burner; hence they first came with two metal handles. Today, flat bottom Woks are commonly equipped with a long wooden handle that resembles a skillet. When stir-frying, the long handle makes it simple to maneuver and tilt the Wok. Most Woks also feature a little "helper" handle on the other side, making it simple to lift them. Round-bottom Woks might have a single long metal or wooden handle or the typical Wok shape with two little metal "ears."

Size Matters

Restaurants use Woks that are several feet large because Woks exist in a variety of sizes. Your personal preferences, the sort of stove you have, and the depth of the Wok will all have an impact on the size of the Wok you select.

Consider Nonstick

Many manufacturers now provide Woks with a nonstick coating due to the current trend toward low-fat cooking. The type of coating used and the method of application will determine how well nonstick functions. Nonstick coatings, however, generally don't work well on carbon steel. Try a strong gauge aluminum Wok, such as those produced by Calphalon, if you want the nonstick coating.

Choose a Wok with a Lid

Why go with a Wok that has a lid? Because cooking Chinese food will be much easier if you have a Wok with a lid. The ingredients frequently need to simmer while being covered during cooking. Therefore, buying a Wok with a lid will make cooking with a Wok much simpler.

Seasoning and Cleaning

A patina is produced by seasoning your cast iron or carbon steel Wok. A well-seasoned Wok will have a smooth nonstick surface and help impart flavors in the foods cooked. Any food cooked in your Wok without seasoning it first is likely to stick and lack flavor.

* Stovetop Technique

A common approach to season your Wok is on the stovetop. For this, a range top burner, some oil, and paper towels are required. To remove factory oil, finish the initial cleaning. If your Wok has wooden handles, either remove them or wrap them in aluminum foil to prevent scorching/burning. To allow the metal's pores to open, preheat the Wok over high heat. Make sure the area around your burner is free of obstructions, your kitchen hood fan is on, and your windows are open because the Wok will become extremely hot and emit smoke.

To heat the front, back, and sides of your Wok, tilt and flip it. The heat will cause your Wok to change color. When the entire surface of your Wok has turned matte and dark, the seasoning procedure is finished. To clean the Wok without removing the seasoning, rinse it with hot water and scrub it with a bamboo Wok brush. Return the Wok to the stovetop and heat it to a high setting to burn out any lingering water droplets. Re-season the Wok if necessary, or store it until you're ready to use it. For a smoother nonstick surface and a thicker protective coating, season the Wok up to three times.

* Seasoning in the Oven

Woks with oven-safe handles are advised to use this technique. Finish the initial cleaning to get rid of factory oil. Set the oven's temperature to 450 degrees Fahrenheit. Aluminum foil is used to line a sheet pan. The outside of the Wok should also be coated with lard, shortening, or oil using a paper towel. Put the lined sheet pan on the oven's bottom rack. On the top rack, put the oiled Wok. After 20 minutes of baking, take the pan out of the oven. Use a soft sponge and warm water to rinse the Wok. On the stovetop, dry it thoroughly using high heat.

* Add Salt to a Wok

Kosher salt is used in this technique to give your Wok a black patina. A pan that hasn't been used in a while can also be revived or re-seasoned using it. Finish the initial cleaning to get rid of factory oil. In a Wok, add 1 cup of kosher salt. On a gas stovetop, place a Wok with salt inside and turn the heat to high. During the 20 minutes of continuous stirring, salt is pushed up and around the sides of the pan. Remove the Wok from the heat after 20 minutes, then pour the heated salt into the sink (letting it cool before you discard it). Spread some oil on the Wok's surface and use an oil-covered rag or paper towel to clean it up.

Setting up a Wok-Friendly Pantry with Supplies

Your pantry must have the following few essentials to add the desired depth of flavors and aroma to your Chinese food.

Sweet Soy Sauce: The most recognizable and well-known Chinese pantry staple that you probably already have on hand is soy sauce. This item is used in so many Chinese recipes, and nowadays, many western chefs keep soy sauce in their cupboards to give their food a richer umami flavor. While soy sauce is a ubiquitous table condiment used by both Asians and

Westerners, you might be surprised to hear that soy sauces from different places, such as Thailand, Japan, and China, differ in taste, saltiness, and color. Everyone has their preferred brands, just like everything else.

Dark Soy Sauce: Regular/light and dark soy sauces are essential to keep on hand for your everyday Chinese pantry. While you can get by with just standard or "light" soy sauce in some recipes, dark soy sauce is essential for other foods to have the proper depth of flavor, color, and consistency!

Sesame Oil: One of the most distinctive tastes of Chinese and Asian cuisine is sesame oil. The majority of sesame oils you see in markets have been roasted, giving them a dark amber hue and a potent scent. Sesame oil in a clear or yellow bottle has almost certainly not been toasted and will not likely have the same robust flavor and aroma.

Oyster Sauce: Whether you're buying the traditional version made from oysters or the vegetarian version made from mushrooms, oyster sauce provides an umami flavor that really elevates the taste of any Chinese dish.

Cornstarch: The most popular thickener used in Chinese cooking is cornstarch, sometimes known as maize flour in some regions. Plus, it is the ingredient that is easiest to find.

Ground White Pepper: In Asian cookery, white pepper is frequently used in place of black pepper, although it is rarely used in Western food. Pre-ground white pepper works just as well in virtually all situations; however, freshly ground white pepper always has a stronger flavor. Its powdery texture is preferred for several uses.

Garlic: Everyone is familiar with garlic, but when making Chinese food, you can never have too much of it on hand!

Ginger: Ginger has a distinct flavor and is used in numerous well-known seafood dishes. For a genuinely authentic flavor, caramelizing ginger slices in the oil gives meals a toasty ginger flavor that permeates the entire dish.

Scallions: Green onions, often known as scallions, are frequently used in Chinese cuisine. This is a familiar component, no doubt, but our Chinese Aromatics page has more advice on how to purchase, store, and use scallions.

Conclusion

Ever since I started using Wok for cooking traditional Chinese recipes, it has somehow become easier to cook delectable stir-fries, seared meat, tofu, steamed fish, and a variety of noodles. And you don't have to be a pro-chef to do so; just a good Wok and some ingredients will do the job. You just have to use the right Wok'ing technique, the instructions in the recipes, and the suggested cooking time. And just like that, your WOK-Fresh cooked meal will then be ready to serve at the table.

Asian Teriyaki Cauliflower and Kale, page 9

Garlic Broccoli, page 12

Simple Stir-Fried Tomato and Eggs, page 14

Garlic Eggplant, page 8

Chapter 3 Vegetables and Sides   7

Chapter 3 Vegetables and Sides

Stir-Fried Bean Sprouts with Carrot

Prep Time: 5 minutes, Cook Time: 5 minutes, Serves: 4 to 6

INGREDIENTS:
4 cups fresh mung bean sprouts, rinsed
½ carrot, julienned
¼ cup chopped garlic chives (1-inch pieces)
1 garlic clove, minced
1 tbsp. peanut oil
2 tsps. soy sauce
Pinch ground white pepper

DIRECTIONS:
1. Heat the peanut oil in a wok over high heat.
2. Place the garlic and stir-fry for just a few seconds until fragrant.
3. Put the carrot and stir-fry for 2 or 3 seconds.
4. Toss the bean sprouts and soy sauce into the wok. Stir well for a few seconds then turn off the heat.
5. Place the garlic chives and pepper at the last minute, and transfer to a serving bowl. Serve warm.

Bok Choy with Ginger

Prep Time: 5 minutes, Cook Time: 5 minutes, Serves: 4 to 6

INGREDIENTS:
4 heads bok choy, cut into bite-size pieces
1-inch piece ginger, peeled and julienned
2 garlic cloves, thinly sliced or minced
1 tbsp. olive oil
1 tbsp. Shaoxing wine
½ tsp. chicken stock granules

DIRECTIONS:
1. Add the olive oil in a cold wok then place the garlic and ginger.
2. Turn the heat to medium-high. When the garlic becomes brown just a little, put the bok choy and stir-fry for a few seconds.
3. Pour in the Shaoxing wine, which will help steam the bok choy. Then add a little water if needed.
4. Season the bok choy with chicken stock granules and stir well.
5. When the stems of the bok choy are soft, they are ready to eat.

Grape Chutney with Herbes

Prep Time: 10 minutes, Cook Time: 10 minutes, Serves: 1

INGREDIENTS:
4 cups red seedless grapes
½ cup chopped red onion
2 tbsps. balsamic vinegar
1 tbsp. butter
1 tsp. fresh rosemary, snipped
¼ tsp. dried oregano, crumbled

DIRECTIONS:
1. In a large wok, melt butter and sauté the onion for about 5 minutes.
2. Place the rosemary and oregano and sauté for about 1 minute.
3. At the same time in a food processor, put the grapes and pulse till chopped roughly.
4. Pour in the vinegar and chopped grapes and cook for 1 to 2 minutes or till heated completely.

Garlic Eggplant

Prep Time: 10 minutes, Cook Time: 10 minutes, Serves: 4

INGREDIENTS:
SAUCE:
2 tbsps. soy sauce
1½ tbsps. Chinese black vinegar or apple cider vinegar
2 tsps. chili bean paste
1½ tsps. brown sugar
1 tsp. dark soy sauce

STIR-FRY:
2 Chinese or Japanese eggplant, cut into bite-size pieces
4 garlic cloves, minced
1 scallion, chopped
3 tbsps. peanut oil
1 tsp. cornstarch

DIRECTIONS:
1. Prepare the sauce by mixing together the soy sauce, vinegar, dark soy sauce, brown sugar, and chili bean paste in a small bowl. Set it aside.
2. Coat the eggplant with a light layer of cornstarch.
3. Heat the peanut oil in a wok over medium-high heat.
4. Stir-fry the eggplant until cooked almost all the way through.
5. Place the garlic and stir-fry until fragrant.
6. Pour the sauce to the wok, stir-frying until all the ingredients are mixed, then remove from the heat.
7. Take the eggplant to a serving dish and garnish with the chopped scallion. Serve hot.

Mediterranean Baby Bok Choy

Prep Time: 15 minutes, Cook Time: 15 minutes, Serves: 4

INGREDIENTS:
- 4 heads baby bok choy
- ¼ cup water
- 1 dash fresh lemon juice
- 3 tbsps. olive oil
- 2 tbsps. balsamic vinegar
- 2 tbsps. capers
- 1½ tsps. minced fresh ginger root
- 1½ tsps. minced garlic

DIRECTIONS:
1. Separate the leaves from the stems of the baby bok choy.
2. Chop the stems into bite-sized chunks and shred the leaves.
3. In a large wok over medium heat, heat the olive oil and cook the bok choy stems for 3 minutes.
4. Pour in the water and leaves and cook for 10 minutes.
5. Stir in the capers, ginger and garlic and cook for about 1 minute more.
6. Pour in the vinegar and lemon juice and remove from the heat.
7. Serve warm.

Asian Teriyaki Cauliflower and Kale

Prep Time: 15 minutes, Cook Time: 10 minutes, Serves: 4

INGREDIENTS:
- 1 pound (454 g) florets of cauliflower
- 1 package baby kale
- ½ cup pineapple juice
- 2 big garlic cloves
- 1 chili pepper
- 2 tbsps. sesame seeds, roasted
- 1½ tbsps. tamari
- 1 tbsp. sesame oil, unrefined
- 1 tbsp. avocado oil
- 1 tsps. ginger root
- Salt and pepper as per your taste

DIRECTIONS:
1. In a bowl, mix together all the spices and liquid ingredients.
2. Heat oil in a wok. Cook the vegetables in it, while occasionally stirring, until the cauliflower becomes browned.
3. Add seasonings as per your taste.
4. Pour the prepared mixture and all other remaining ingredients.
5. Serve hot.

Simple Cambodia Corn

Prep Time: 5 minutes, Cook Time: 20 minutes, Serves: 6

INGREDIENTS:
- Vegetable oil, for coating
- 6 ears corn, husks and silk removed
- 2 green onions, white parts only, sliced
- 2 tbsps. vegetable oil
- 2 tbsps. fish sauce
- 2 tbsps. water
- 1½ tbsps. sugar
- 1 tsp. salt

DIRECTIONS:
1. Use a little oil to coat the corn ears.
2. Heat a cast-iron wok over medium heat until heated through.
3. Place the corn and cook for 13 to 15 minutes, flipping after every 3 minutes.
4. Take the corn from the heat and transfer onto a platter.
5. Cover the corn with a piece of foil to keep warm.
6. Add the sugar, fish sauce, salt and water in a bowl, and mix until well combined.
7. In a wok over medium heat, pour in 2 tbsps. of the oil and cook until just heated.
8. Place the green onions and sugar mixture and cook for 40 seconds, stirring frequently.
9. Remove from the heat and set aside to cool.
10. Coat the corn with the sauce and enjoy.

Curry Veggie Caribbean Style

Prep Time: 20 minutes, Cook Time: 35 minutes, Serves: 6

INGREDIENTS:
- 2 potatoes, cut into small cubes
- 1 cup chopped bok choy
- 1 plantains, peeled and broken into chunks
- ½ cup chopped broccoli
- ½ cup chopped red bell pepper
- 1 small onion, chopped
- 4 cloves garlic, minced
- ¼ cup olive oil
- 1 cup water
- 1 tbsp. grated fresh ginger root
- 1 tsp. ground cumin
- ½ tsp. ground turmeric
- ½ tsp. curry powder
- ½ tsp. ground allspice
- Salt to taste

DIRECTIONS:
1. Mix together the cumin, turmeric, allspice and curry powder in a small bowl.
2. In a wok on medium-low heat, heat the olive oil and sauté the ginger and cumin mixture for 5 minutes.
3. Place the onion and garlic and cook for about 1 to 2 minutes.
4. Toss in the potatoes and cook for 1 to 2 minutes.
5. Put the red bell pepper, bok choy, broccoli, plantains and enough water to reach about half-full and simmer, covered for 20 to 25 minutes.
6. Sprinkle with the salt and serve warm.

Chinese North Bok Choy

Prep Time: 15 minutes, Cook Time: 10 minutes, Serves: 4

INGREDIENTS:
½ pound (227 g) baby bok choy, trimmed and chopped
3 dried red chili peppers, seeded and thinly sliced
¼ cup vegetable oil
3 tbsps. cold water
1½ tbsps. white sugar
1½ tbsps. cornstarch
1 tbsp. brown rice vinegar
Salt to taste

DIRECTIONS:
1. Mix together the sugar, brown rice vinegar, cornstarch and cold water in a bowl.
2. In a large wok over high heat, heat the oil and cook the chili peppers for about 4 minutes.
3. Transfer the chili peppers into a bowl with a slotted spoon.
4. Add the bok choy and sauté for 1 to 2 minutes.
5. Pour in the vinegar sauce and bring to a boil.
6. Cook for another 30 seconds.
7. Transfer to a plate and season with the salt.

Tianjin Stir Fry Vegetables

Prep Time: 15 minutes, Cook Time: 15 minutes, Serves: 2

INGREDIENTS:
3½ ounces (99 g) bok choy
3½ ounces (99 g) daikon radishes, thinly sliced
3 ounces (85 g) carrots, peeled and thinly sliced
2 cremini mushrooms, thinly sliced
1 small beet, peeled and thinly sliced
1 tbsp. butter
¼ tsp. ground cardamom

DIRECTIONS:
1. In a wok over medium-high heat, melt the butter. Sauté the beet, carrots, daikon radishes and mushrooms for 5 minutes.
2. Cover the wok.
3. Chop the bottom half off bok choy. Then slice the bok choy leaves into ribbons.
4. Place the chopped bok choy into the wok and cook for 5 minutes.
5. Stir in the bok choy leaves and cardamom and cook for about 1 minute more. Serve warm.

Asian Wok Sticky Tofu and Veggies

Prep Time: 30 minutes, Cook Time: 10 minutes, Serves: 2

INGREDIENTS:
1 packet of tofu
1 cup lettuce, shredded
½ cup rice noodles
½ cup carrots, thinly sliced or shredded
½ cup red cabbage shredded, or red cabbage selected
½ cup cucumbers, sliced thinly
1 handful of chopped cilantro
1 avocado, in slices
2 tbsps. hoisin sauce
1 tbsp. avocado oil
1 tbsp. Sriracha
1 tbsp. soy sauce
Seeds of sesame for topping

DIRECTIONS:
1. Start with the sticky tofu being packed.
2. Cut the tofu into cubes and put in a hot wok with the oil on medium-high heat.
3. Enable 3 to 5 minutes to tan and then gently flip the cubes on either side to brown.
4. Turn off the heat and stir in the hoisin sauce, soy sauce, and Sriracha until each side becomes golden brown and crispy.
5. Cook the rice noodles according to the instructions in the package.
6. Serve it warm with veggies and noodles.

Asian Wok Veggies with Peanut Butter Sauce

Prep Time: 20 minutes, Cook Time: 15 minutes, Serves: 4

INGREDIENTS:
SAUCE:
½ cup water
2 tbsps. peanut butter
2 tbsps. chile sauce
2 tbsps. soy sauce
1 tbsp. maple syrup
STIR-FRY:
1 pound (454 g) snow peas
3 cups fresh or frozen veggies
1 onion, chopped
3½ ounces (99 g) glass noodles
A handful of corns
1 tbsp. oil
1 garlic clove
1 ginger root

DIRECTIONS:
1. Defrost the frozen vegetables and chopped.
2. In a large mixing basin, mix together the peanut butter, sweet chili sauce, soy sauce, water, and syrup, with a spoon until it is a lovely, creamy sauce.
3. Cook the noodles according to the instructions in the package. Drain and rinse under cold water when cooked.
4. Heat the oil in a wok over high heat. Add the garlic, ginger, onion, snow snaps and corn in it.
5. Place vegetables in it and sauté them.
6. Reduce the heat to medium-low and toss in the sauce and noodles.
7. Let simmer for another 3 to 5 minutes. Serve warm.

Stir-Fried Bok Choy

Prep Time: 5 minutes, Cook Time: 5 minutes, Serves: 4

INGREDIENTS:
- 5 heads baby bok choy, ends trimmed and leaves separated
- 1 clove garlic, minced
- 2 tbsps. water
- 1 tbsp. olive oil
- 1 tsp. minced fresh ginger root

DIRECTIONS:
1. In a large wok over high heat, heat the oil. Sauté the garlic and ginger for about 30 seconds.
2. Stir in the baby bok choy and water and cook, covered for 2 minutes. Serve warm.

Luncheon Brussels Sprouts with Broccoli

Prep Time: 15 minutes, Cook Time: 10 minutes, Serves: 6

INGREDIENTS:
- 8 Brussels sprouts, trimmed and halved
- 2 cups broccoli florets
- 1 small tomato, seeded and diced
- 2 cloves garlic, chopped
- 3 tbsps. butter, divided
- ¼ tsp. salt
- ⅛ tsp. red pepper flakes

DIRECTIONS:
1. In a wok on medium heat, melt 1 tbsp. of the butter and sauté the garlic for 1 to 2 minutes.
2. Place the broccoli and Brussels sprouts, remaining butter, tomato, salt and red pepper flakes and cook, covered for 5 minutes.
3. Frequently flip sprouts and broccoli and cook, covered for 4 minutes. Serve warm.

Suzhou Five Spice Bok Choy with Cashews

Prep Time: 15 minutes, Cook Time: 10 minutes, Serves: 4

INGREDIENTS:
- 1 large head bok choy
- ⅓ cup cashews
- 1 onion, sliced
- 3 cloves garlic, minced
- 1 tbsp. grapeseed oil
- 1 tbsp. butter
- 1 pinch white sugar
- ½ tsp. Chinese five-spice powder

DIRECTIONS:
1. Slice the root-end of bok choy into ½-1-inch slices and discard the stems.
2. Chop the stalks diagonally into ⅛-inch pieces and tear the leaves into bite-sized pieces.
3. In a wok over medium heat, heat the oil and butter. Sauté the onion, garlic, cashews, bok choy, Chinese five-spice and sugar for about 8 to 10 minutes. Serve warm.

Ningbo Stir Fry Vegetables

Prep Time: 30 minutes, Cook Time: 10 minutes, Serves: 6

INGREDIENTS:
- 1 to 1½ pounds (454 to 680 g) bok choy, coarsely chopped
- 3 cups sliced fresh broccoli florets
- 1 medium onion, thinly sliced
- 2 cloves garlic, minced
- 2 tbsps. vegetable oil
- 2 tbsps. lemon juice
- 1 tbsp. freshly grated ginger root
- 1½ tsps. sugar
- ½ tsp. salt
- ¼ tsp. red pepper flakes

DIRECTIONS:
1. In a large wok on medium-high heat, heat the oil and sauté the onion, garlic, ginger, salt and red pepper flakes for 2 minutes.
2. Place the broccoli and bok choy and stir-fry for about 1 to 2 minutes.
3. Pour the lemon juice and sugar and stir-fry for about 3 minutes. Serve warm.

Tasty Vegetarian Tanzanian Skillet

Prep Time: 10 minutes, Cook Time: 30 minutes, Serves: 4

INGREDIENTS:
- 2 pounds (907 g) spinach, chopped
- 1 tomatoes, peeled and chopped
- 1 cup coconut milk
- 1 onion, chopped
- 1½ ounces (43 g) peanut butter
- 3 tbsps. ghee
- 2 tsps. curry powder
- 1 tsp. salt

DIRECTIONS:
1. Whisk the peanut butter and coconut milk in a mixing bowl.
2. In a large wok over medium heat, heat the ghee. Cook the tomato with onion, curry powder and a pinch of salt for about 6 minutes.
3. Toss in the spinach and cook them for 16 to 21 minutes over low heat.
4. Once the time is up, pour in the peanut butter and milk mix. Let them cook for another 6 minutes.
5. Serve warm.

Chapter 3 Vegetables and Sides

Stir-Fried Garlic Spinach

Prep Time: 5 minutes, Cook Time: 5 minutes, Serves: 4

INGREDIENTS:

6 cups fresh spinach, rinsed
4 garlic cloves, thinly sliced or minced
1 tbsp. olive oil
½ tsp. chicken stock granules
Pinch salt

DIRECTIONS:

1. Heat the olive oil in a wok over medium-high heat.
2. Place the garlic and stir-fry until fragrant, just a few seconds.
3. Stir in the spinach, salt and chicken stock granules.
4. Stir-fry the spinach until the leaves wilt.
5. Transfer to a serving dish and serve warm.

Honey Brussels Sprouts

Prep Time: 10 minutes, Cook Time: 15 minutes, Serves: 4

INGREDIENTS:

1 pound (454 g) Brussels sprouts, grated
½ cup chopped onion
¼ cup honey-flavored butter
2 tbsps. white cooking wine
Salt and ground black pepper to taste

DIRECTIONS:

1. In a large wok over medium-high heat, melt the honey-flavored butter and sauté the onion for 5 to 7 minutes.
2. Place the Brussels sprouts, salt and pepper. Sauté sprouts for 5 to 7 minutes.
3. Remove the wok from the heat and pour in the wine and toss to coat. Serve warm.

Basic Stir-Fried Cabbage

Prep Time: 5 minutes, Cook Time: 5 minutes, Serves: 4 to 6

INGREDIENTS:

1 head cabbage, shredded
2 garlic cloves, minced
2 tbsps. soy sauce
1½ tbsps. olive oil
1 tbsp. Shaoxing wine or water
Pinch salt
Pinch ground white pepper

DIRECTIONS:

1. Heat the olive oil in a wok over medium-high heat.
2. Place the garlic, stir-fry for about 20 seconds, and add the cabbage.
3. Stir the cabbage with g a wok spatula for about 1 minute, then pour the Shaoxing wine, soy sauce, salt and pepper.
4. Stir-fry until the cabbage wilt.
5. Remove from the heat and serve hot.

Teriyaki Vegan Combo

Prep Time: 10 minutes, Cook Time: 12 minutes, Serves: 2

INGREDIENTS:

1 large zucchini, cut into long strands
1 large carrot, thinly sliced
1 head baby bok choy, chopped
½ large green bell pepper, thinly sliced
¼ large yellow onion, thinly sliced
2 tbsps. teriyaki sauce, divided
1 tbsp. olive oil
1 tsp. garlic powder

DIRECTIONS:

1. In a large wok over medium heat, heat the olive oil and 1 tbsp. of the teriyaki sauce and sauté the bell pepper, carrot and onion for 5 minutes.
2. Stir in the zucchini, bok choy, garlic powder and remaining teriyaki sauce and cook for 7 minutes, stirring from time to time.

Garlic Broccoli

Prep Time: 5 minutes, Cook Time: 5 minutes, Serves: 6 to 8

INGREDIENTS:

1 pound (454 g) Chinese broccoli (kai lan), rinsed and cut into bite-size pieces
4 garlic cloves, peeled and halved
½ (2-inch) piece ginger, peeled and julienned
2 tbsps. peanut oil
2 tbsps. oyster sauce
1 tsp. sugar
Pinch ground white pepper

DIRECTIONS:

1. Heat the peanut oil in a wok over medium heat.
2. Place the garlic. Once it starts to turn golden brown, put the ginger and give it all a quick stir.
3. Increase the heat to high and quickly add the kai lan, sugar, oyster sauce, and pepper.
4. Toss the kai lan well. Pour in a tbsp. or two of water to help steam it, if desired.
5. When the kai lan becomes bright green and softens a little, remove it from the heat and serve hot.

Chapter 3 Vegetables and Sides

Vegetarian Bok Choy

Prep Time: 10 minutes, Cook Time: 10 minutes, Serves: 4

INGREDIENTS:

8 heads baby bok choy, trimmed and cut into bite-size pieces
2 cloves garlic, crushed and chopped
1 tbsp. vegetable oil
Salt to taste

DIRECTIONS:

1. In a large wok on medium heat, heat the oil and sauté the garlic for 1 to 2 minutes.
2. Stir in the bok choy and sauté for 5 to 8 minutes.
3. Season with the salt and serve hot.

Broccoli with Braised Mushrooms

Prep Time: 10 minutes, Cook Time: 20 minutes, Serves: 6 to 8

INGREDIENTS:

2 cups dried shiitake mushrooms
Water for soaking mushrooms
SAUCE:
¼ cup oyster sauce
¼ cup water, plus 2 tbsps. for cornstarch mixture
1 tbsp. soy sauce
2 tsps. cornstarch
1 tsp. sugar
2 pinches ground white pepper
BROCCOLI:
2 heads broccoli, cut into florets
1 tbsp. sesame oil
1 tbsp. peanut oil

DIRECTIONS:

1. Soak the shiitake mushrooms in water for a few hours or overnight until softened. If time is of the essence, boil them in water for 30 minutes.
2. Rinse the mushrooms, remove their stems and squeeze as much water out of them as possible. Let rest and set aside.
3. Prepare the sauce by combining ¼ cup of water and the oyster sauce, soy sauce, sugar, and pepper in a small bowl. Set it aside.
4. Combine 2 tbsps. of water and the cornstarch in another small bowl. Set it aside.
5. In a wok over high heat, steam the broccoli florets on a metal steaming rack for about 5 minutes. Set them aside and drain the water of the wok.
6. Return the wok to the stove top. Let the wok dry completely. Heat the peanut oil and sesame oil over medium-low heat.
7. Place the sauce and mushrooms to the wok. Simmer for 10 minutes, stirring occasionally.
8. Increase the heat to high, and pour in the cornstarch-water mixture, stirring to thicken the sauce.
9. Arrange the broccoli on a round plate in a circle along the edge. Pour the mushrooms and sauce in the center of the plate, and serve warm.

Healthy Baby Romaine with Goji Berries

Prep Time: 5 minutes, Cook Time: 5 minutes, Serves: 4 to 6

INGREDIENTS:

2 heads baby romaine lettuce
¼ cup dried goji berries
2 garlic cloves, minced
1 tbsp. olive oil
2 tsps. Shaoxing wine
1 tsp. chicken stock granules
Pinch salt

DIRECTIONS:

1. Separate the romaine leaves, rinse and drain well.
2. Heat the olive oil in a wok over high heat.
3. Add the garlic, lettuce leaves, goji berries, chicken stock granules, salt and Shaoxing wine, stirring occasionally.
4. Give all the ingredients a quick stir. Transfer to a serving plate and serve hot.

Brussels Sprouts with Pistachios

Prep Time: 15 minutes, Cook Time: 15 minutes, Serves: 6

INGREDIENTS:

4 pounds (1.8 kg) Brussels sprouts
½ cup coarsely chopped pistachios
4 small red onions, cut into strips
½ cup unsalted butter
¼ cup red wine vinegar
2 tbsps. white sugar
Salt and pepper to taste

DIRECTIONS:

1. Set a steamer basket in a pan of the boiling water.
2. In the steamer basket, place the Brussels sprouts and cook, covered for 8 to 10
3. minutes.
4. In a deep wok on medium heat, melt the butter and cook the onions and 3 tbsps. of the vinegar till the onions become browned.
5. Place the Brussels sprouts, sugar and remaining vinegar and cook till the Brussels sprouts are lightly caramelized.
6. Sprinkle with the salt and pepper and transfer to a plate.
7. Garnish with the pistachios and serve.

Maple Brussels Sprouts Stir Fry

Prep Time: 15 minutes, Cook Time: 10 minutes, Serves: 1

INGREDIENTS:
3 Brussels sprouts, trimmed, halved lengthwise, and thinly sliced
2½ tsps. chopped dried apricots
1 tsp. lime juice
1 tsp. water
¾ tsp. maple syrup
½ tsp. butter

DIRECTIONS:
1. In a wok on medium-high heat, melt the butter and cook the sprouts, apricot, water and maple syrup for 5 to 10 minutes.
2. Stir in the lime juice and quickly transfer to a serving plate. Serve warm.

Simple Stir-Fried Tomato and Eggs

Prep Time: 5 minutes, Cook Time: 5 minutes, Serves: 4 to 6

INGREDIENTS:
2 medium tomatoes, cut into wedges
4 eggs
1 scallion, cut into 1-inch pieces
2 tbsps. peanut oil
1 tsp. Shaoxing wine
½ tsp. sugar
Pinch salt
Pinch pepper

DIRECTIONS:
1. Add the eggs and the Shaoxing wine in a medium bowl. Season with salt and pepper and beat together until combined well.
2. Heat the peanut oil in a wok over medium-high heat.
3. Pour the egg mixture into the wok and let the bottom cook before gently scrambling.
4. Just before the egg starts to cook all the way through, take it from the wok.
5. Toss the tomato wedges into the wok and stir-fry until they become a little tender.
6. Take the scrambled eggs back to the wok with the tomato, then add the sugar over the stir-fry.
7. Turn off the heat, sprinkle the scallion and give one last stir before transferring to a serving plate. Serve warm.

Healthy Black Beans with Apples, page 19

Asian Yellow Peas with Spinach, page 17

Mexican Wok Black Beans and Zucchinis, page 18

Quinoa Fried Rice with Beans, page 19

Chapter 4 Beans and Legume

Chapter 4 Beans and Legume

Authentic Beans Caprese

Prep Time: 15 minutes, Cook Time: 15 minutes, Serves: 1

INGREDIENTS:

1½ pounds (680 g) green beans
½ pint cherry tomatoes, halved
1 tbsp. butter
1 tbsp. sugar
½ tsp. basil
¾ tsp. garlic salt
Salt and pepper

DIRECTIONS:

1. Put a large saucepan of water over high heat. Heat it until it starts boiling.
2. Add the green beans and cook for 7 minutes until they become tender. Drain them.
3. In a large wok over medium heat, heat the butter until it melts.
4. Place the garlic salt, sugar, basil, salt and pepper with cherry tomatoes and cook for 3 minutes.
5. Toss in the green beans and cook them for another 2 minutes.
6. Serve hot.

Ginger Orange Lentil Stew

Prep Time: 10 minutes, Cook Time: 35 minutes, Serves: 6

INGREDIENTS:

2 cups orange lentils, rinsed
1 cup fresh tomato, diced peeled
1 large sweet onion, chopped
3 garlic cloves, crushed
1 inch piece fresh ginger, grated
¼ cup vegetable oil
1 tsp. cumin seed, crushed
1 tsp. cardamom seed, crushed
1 tsp. coriander powder
1 tsp. turmeric
¼ tsp. ground cinnamon
½ tsp. salt
½ tsp. cayenne pepper

DIRECTIONS:

1. Put a large saucepan over medium heat. Stir in the lentils with a pinch of salt. Cover them with boiling water.
2. Cook the lentils for about 22 minutes.
3. Once the time is up, drain the lentils. Arrange it in a mixing bowl and use a potato masher to mash it slightly.
4. In a large wok over medium heat, heat the oil. Cook the onion and garlic for 5 minutes.
5. Toss in the rest of ingredients and cook for 6 minutes. Place the lentils and heat them through.
6. Serve warm.

Seared Tofu with Green Beans and Coconut Sauce

Prep Time: 25 minutes, Cook Time: 15 minutes, Serves: 4

INGREDIENTS:

1 pound (454 g) green beans
1 package firm tofu, chopped
1 can unsweetened coconut milk
½ cup salted roasted cashews, chopped
1 red bell pepper, thinly sliced
Rice noodles or rice
¼ cup vegetable oil
2 tbsps. soy sauce
1 tbsp. garlic, coarsely diced
1 tbsp. fresh ginger, peeled and chopped
1 tbsp. lime zest
Half spicy red pepper flakes (dry)
Salt and pepper as per your taste

DIRECTIONS:

1. Put the chopped tofu in a dish then pour soy sauce over it. Allow it to marinate for ten minutes.
2. In a wok over medium heat, heat the oil until it is hot but not scorching, then arrange the tofu in 1 layer and cook until it turned brown or for about 5 minutes total.
3. Remove to a large dish with a spoon, retaining the oil in the pan.
4. Place the spices and minced garlic to the wok and let it cook until it turns aromatic.
5. Put the bell pepper, beans, and minced ginger. Cook while stirring frequently.
6. Bring the coconut milk and remaining tbsp. of soy sauce to a boil, reduce to low heat, cook for about 6 minutes or until the beans are tender.
7. Transfer the veggies and the tofu to the platter with a spoon.
8. Cook until the sauce has thickened slightly and been reduced to only ¾ cup, about 2 minutes.
9. Add the sauce over the veggies and tofu after adding the lime zest.
10. Top with cashews.
11. Serve warm with rice noodles or rice.

Saucy Green Beans Skillet

Prep Time: 5 minutes, Cook Time: 15 minutes, Serves: 4

INGREDIENTS:
14 ounces (397 g) green beans, trimmed and halved
1 tomato, diced
1 tbsp. olive oil
1 tsp. chopped garlic
Salt and pepper

DIRECTIONS:
1. Place a saucepan of salted water over medium heat and bring it to a boil.
2. Cook the beans for 9 minutes then drain them.
3. In a wok, heat the oil over medium heat. Cook the garlic for 35 seconds.
4. Add the beans and cook for about 2 to 3 minutes.
5. Stir in the tomato with a pinch of salt and pepper. Cook them for about 4 minutes.
6. Serve warm.

Asian Yellow Peas with Spinach

Prep Time: 30 minutes, Cook Time: 40 minutes, Serves: 5

INGREDIENTS:
2 cups yellow split peas
8 ounces (227 g) spinach, washed and coarsely chopped
1 medium chili serrano, stemmed and thinly chopped
5 big garlic cloves, peeled and finely minced
¼ cup fresh ginger, peeled and finely chopped
8 cups water
8 tsps. butter unsalted
2 tsps. freshly squeezed lemon juice
2 tsps. cumin seeds
1½ tsps. turmeric
2 tsps. salt, plus more as required

DIRECTIONS:
1. In a fine-mesh strainer, arrange the split peas and rinse them vigorously under cold water. Transfer to a wide saucepan, pour in the water you have weighed, and bring to a boil over high heat.
2. Reduce the heat to medium-low and simmer for about 30 minutes, using a large spoon to stir and skim any scum off the surface until the peas are completely soft and the consistency of split pea soup thickens.
3. Set aside, remove from the heat, and place the lemon juice and the measured salt in it.
4. In a wok over medium heat, heat the butter until it is foamed. Place the cumin seeds and turmeric in it and simmer for around 3 minutes, until the cumin seeds are toasted and fragrant and the butter is very foamy, stirring periodically.
5. Put the garlic, ginger and serrano and season with salt. Simmer for 2 to 3 minutes, stirring occasionally, until the vegetables are soft. Place the spinach and simmer until the spinach is entirely wilted, stirring occasionally, for around 4 minutes.
6. Transfer the spinach mixture to the reserved saucepan with the split peas, and mix to blend. Serve warm.

Green Bean with Chicken Thighs

Prep Time: 15 minutes, Cook Time: 15 minutes, Serves: 4

INGREDIENTS:
¾ pound (340 g) green beans, trimmed and halved crosswise diagonally
¾ pound (340 g) boneless, skinless chicken thighs, sliced across the grain into bite-size strips
¼ cup slivered almonds, toasted
4 peeled fresh ginger slices, each about the size of a quarter
3 tbsps. Shaoxing rice wine, divided
3 tbsps. vegetable oil, divided
2 tbsps. light soy sauce
1 tbsp. seasoned rice vinegar
2 tsps. sesame oil
2 tsps. cornstarch
Kosher salt
Red pepper flakes

DIRECTIONS:
1. Combine the chicken with 1 tbsp. of rice wine, cornstarch, a small pinch of salt, and a pinch of red pepper flakes in a mixing bowl. Stir to coat the chicken evenly. Marinate for about 10 minutes.
2. Heat a wok over high heat until a drop of water sizzles and evaporates on contact. Add 2 tbsps. of vegetable oil and swirl to coat the base of the wok well. Season the oil with the ginger and a small pinch of salt. Let the ginger sizzle in the oil for 30 seconds, swirling slowly.
3. Place the chicken and marinade to the wok and stir-fry for about 3 to 4 minutes, or until the chicken is slightly seared and no longer pink. Take to a clean bowl and set aside.
4. Pour in the remaining 1 tbsp. of vegetable oil and stir-fry the green beans for 2 to 3 minutes, or until they become bright green. Take the chicken back to the wok and toss together. Add the remaining 2 tbsps. of rice wine, vinegar and light soy. Toss to combine and coat well. Let the green beans simmer for 3 more minutes, or until the green beans are soft. Remove the ginger and throw away.
5. Sprinkle with the almonds and transfer to a platter. Drizzle with the sesame oil and serve warm.

Venetian Garlic Beans

Prep Time: 10 minutes, Cook Time: 11 minutes, Serves: 5

INGREDIENTS:

2 (15-ounce / 425-g) cans cut green beans, drained
¼ cup Italian style bread crumbs
2 to 3 cloves garlic, pressed
2 tbsps. butter

DIRECTIONS:

1. In a wok over medium heat, heat the butter.
2. Cook the beans and garlic for about 11 minutes. Stir in the bread crumbs and turn off the heat.
3. Season as your taste and serve it warm.

Noodles with Green Beans and Cabbage

Prep Time: 15 minutes, Cook Time: 10 minutes, Serves: 4

INGREDIENTS:

½ pound (227 g) dried sweet potato noodles or mung bean noodles
½ pound (227 g) green beans, trimmed and halved
1 small head napa cabbage, chopped into bite-size pieces
3 scallions, coarsely chopped
2 peeled fresh ginger slices, each about the size of a quarter
2 tbsps. vegetable oil
2 tbsps. light soy sauce
1 tbsp. oyster sauce
2 tsps. dark soy sauce
1 tsp. sugar
Kosher salt
1 tsp. Sichuan peppercorns

DIRECTIONS:

1. In a large bowl, soak the noodles in hot water for 10 minutes to soften them. Gently drain the noodles in a colander. Rinse with cold water and let rest.
2. Mix together the light soy, dark soy, oyster sauce and sugar in a small bowl. Set aside.
3. Heat a wok over high heat until a drop of water sizzles and evaporates on contact. Add the oil and swirl to coat the base of the wok well. Season the oil with the ginger, a small pinch of salt and the Sichuan peppercorns. Let the ginger sizzle in the oil for about 30 seconds, swirling slowly. Remove the ginger and peppercorns and discard.
4. Place the napa cabbage and green beans to the wok and stir-fry, tossing and flipping for about 3 to 4 minutes, until the vegetables wilt. Stir in the sauce and toss to combine well.
5. Put the noodles and toss to combine with the sauce and vegetables. Cover the lid and lower the heat to medium. Cook for about 2 to 3 minutes, or until the noodles become transparent and the green beans are tender.
6. Increase the heat to medium-high and uncover the wok. Stir-fry, tossing and scooping for extra 1 to 2 minutes, until the sauce thickens slightly. Remove from the heat and garnish with the scallions. Serve warm.

Caramelized Balsamic Bean with Onion

Prep Time: 5 minutes, Cook Time: 16 minutes, Serves: 4

INGREDIENTS:

1 pound (454 g) green beans, trimmed and halved
1 medium red onion wedges
1 cup water
2 tbsps. olive oil
2 tsps. balsamic vinegar
1 tsp. salt
¼ tsp. ground pepper

DIRECTIONS:

1. In a wok over medium heat, heat the oil. Add 1 cup water, salt and pepper until they start simmering.
2. Toss in onion with green beans. Cover the lid and cook for about 9 minutes.
3. Once the time is up, uncover the lid. Cook for another 7 minutes.
4. Pour in vinegar and stir to coat well. Serve warm.

Mexican Wok Black Beans and Zucchinis

Prep Time: 20 minutes, Cook Time: 15 minutes, Serves: 4

INGREDIENTS:

1 (15-ounce / 425-g) can black beans, rinsed and drained
4 small zucchinis, diced
1 cup frozen whole kernel corn
1 large onion, chopped
1 fresh poblano chili pepper, seeded and chopped
3 cloves garlic, minced
1 tbsp. olive oil
½ tsp. salt

DIRECTIONS:

1. In a large wok on medium-high heat, heat the oil and cook the onion and garlic until soft.
2. Place the zucchinis and poblano pepper and cook till tender.
3. Stir in the corn and black beans and cook till heated entirely.
4. Season with the salt to taste and serve warm.

Curry Garbanzo with Tomato

Prep Time: 10 minutes, Cook Time: 20 minutes, Serves: 4

INGREDIENTS:

1 (16-ounce / 454-g) cans garbanzo beans
½ cup tomatoes, diced
1 onion, diced
Coriander leaves
1 tbsp. ghee
1 tsp. coriander powder
1 tsp. garam masala
1 tsp. chili powder
1 tsp. ginger, grated
1 tsp. garlic, minced
1 tsp. cumin powder
1 tsp. turmeric
Lemon slices for serving

DIRECTIONS:

1. In a wok, heat the ghee over medium heat.
2. Add garlic, onion and ginger and cook for 6 minutes.
3. Toss in the tomatoes, cumin, coriander, turmeric, chili powder and salt.
4. Cook for about 6 minutes. Stir in the garbanzo beans and cook them for about 3 minutes.
5. Put the garam masala and cook for about 2 minutes.
6. Season as your taste. Serve it hot with some lemon slices.

Quinoa Fried Rice with Beans

Prep Time: 10 minutes, Cook Time: 5 minutes, Serves: 4 to 6

INGREDIENTS:

6 cups cooked quinoa
1 cup frozen peas and carrots (no need to thaw)
3 or 4 string beans, cut into ¼-inch pieces
2 eggs, lightly beaten
3 garlic cloves, minced
1 scallion, chopped
2 tbsps. peanut oil
2 tbsps. soy sauce

DIRECTIONS:

1. In a wok, heat the peanut oil over medium-high heat.
2. In the wok, scramble the eggs until cooked, then take them to a small bowl.
3. Place the garlic to the wok and stir-fry for 20 seconds. Put the string beans and stir-fry for about 20 to 30 seconds.
4. Pour in more peanut oil if necessary, then arrange the peas and carrots and stir-fry for 30 seconds.
5. Place the quinoa and return the scrambled egg to the wok, stirring to combine well.
6. Toss in the soy sauce. Stir-fry gently to combine with a wok spatula.
7. Transfer to a serving dish and top with the chopped scallion.

Healthy Black Beans with Apples

Prep Time: 15 minutes, Cook Time: 5 minutes, Serves: 4

INGREDIENTS:

2 (15-ounce / 425-g) cans black beans, rinsed and drained
2 Granny Smith apples, unpeeled, cored and chopped
1 onion, diced
1 red bell pepper, chopped
2 tbsps. lemon juice
2 tbsps. chopped fresh cilantro
1 tbsp. canola oil
2 tsps. ground cumin
½ tsp. salt
⅛ tsp. cayenne pepper

DIRECTIONS:

1. In a large wok on medium heat, heat the oil and sauté the onion and bell pepper for 5 minutes.
2. Toss in the cumin, salt and cayenne pepper and remove from the heat.
3. Take the mixture into a bowl with black beans, cilantro, apples and lemon juice and mix well.
4. Refrigerate to chill before serving.

Alexandria Nutty Rice Casserole, page 22

Couscous Ghardaïa with Mushroom, page 22

Basmati Rice with Cashews, page 23

Vegetable Egg Fried Rice, page 25

20   Chapter 5 Grain and Rice

Chapter 5 Grain and Rice

Spam Pineapple Fried Rice

Prep Time: 5 minutes, Cook Time: 15 minutes, Serves: 4

INGREDIENTS:

1 (12-ounce / 340-g) can Spam, cut into ½-inch cubes
3 cups cold cooked rice
½ cup canned pineapple chunks, juices reserved
½ cup frozen peas and carrots
½ white onion, cut to ¼-inch cubes
2 garlic cloves, finely minced
2 peeled fresh ginger slices, each about the size of a quarter
2 scallions, thinly sliced, divided
3 tbsps. unsalted butter
2 tbsps. light soy sauce
1 tbsp. sesame oil
1 tbsp. vegetable oil
1 tsp. sriracha
1 tsp. light brown sugar
Kosher salt

DIRECTIONS:

1. Heat a wok over high heat until a drop of water sizzles and evaporates on contact. Add the vegetable oil and swirl to coat the base of the wok well. Season the oil with the ginger and a small pinch of salt. Let the ginger sizzle in the oil for about 30 seconds, swirling slowly.
2. Place the diced Spam and evenly spread it out across the bottom of the wok. Let the Spam sear before tossing and flipping. Continue to stir-fry the Spam for about 5 to 6 minutes, until it becomes golden and crispy around all sides.
3. Put the onion and garlic and stir-fry for 2 minutes, until the onion begins to turn translucent. Arrange the peas and carrots and half the scallions. Stir-fry for 1 minute more.
4. Toss in the rice and pineapple, breaking up any large clumps of rice, then toss and flip to combine all of the ingredients well. Stir-fry for about 1 minute, then push it all to the sides of the wok, creating a well in the bottom of the wok.
5. Pour in the butter, reserved pineapple juice, sriracha, light soy and brown sugar. Stir to dissolve the sugar entirely and bring the sauce to a boil, then cook for 1 minute to reduce the sauce and thicken it slightly. Combine everything to coat well, about 30 seconds.
6. Spread the fried rice evenly in the wok and allow the rice to sit against the wok to crisp up slightly, about 2 minutes. Scoop out the ginger and discard. Drizzle with sesame oil and season with a small pinch of salt. Remove from heat and garnish with the remaining scallions. Serve hot.

Indian Fried Rice with Onion

Prep Time: 10 minutes, Cook Time: 4 minutes, Serves: 4

INGREDIENTS:

2 cups cold, cooked basmati rice
¼ cup coarsely chopped mint leaves
1 medium onion, diced
2 garlic cloves, crushed and chopped
2 bird's eye chiles, sliced into ¼-inch circles
2 tbsps. cooking oil
1 tbsp. ginger, crushed and chopped
1 tsp. mustard seeds
1 tsp. hot sesame oil
½ tsp. turmeric
½ tsp. ground coriander
¼ tsp. kosher salt

DIRECTIONS:

1. In a wok, heat the cooking oil over high heat until it shimmers.
2. Add the onion, ginger, mustard seeds and garlic to the wok and stir-fry for about 1 minute.
3. Place the bird's eye chiles, sesame oil, coriander, turmeric, salt and rice and stir-fry for 1 minute.
4. Sprinkle with the mint and serve hot.

Japanese Fried Rice with Bacon

Prep Time: 15 minutes, Cook Time: 8 minutes, Serves: 4

INGREDIENTS:

2 cups cold, cooked rice
½ pound (227 g) thick-sliced bacon, cut into 1-inch pieces
3 eggs, beaten
4 scallions, cut into ½-inch pieces
2 garlic cloves, crushed and chopped
2 tbsps. sesame seeds
1 tbsp. ginger, crushed and chopped
1 tsp. sesame oil
Kosher salt
Ground black pepper

DIRECTIONS:

1. In a wok over high heat, stir-fry the bacon, garlic and ginger for about 2 minutes, or till the bacon is lightly browned.
2. Transfer the bacon to a bowl and set aside.
3. Add the eggs and stir-fry until they are firm and dry.
4. Toss in the cooked bacon, rice and sesame oil and stir-fry for about 1 minute.
5. Put the sesame seeds and scallions and toss for 30 seconds.
6. Season with salt and pepper to taste. Serve warm.

Couscous Ghardaïa with Mushroom

Prep Time: 15 minutes, Cook Time: 15 minutes, Serves: 6

INGREDIENTS:
- 1 cup couscous
- 1 grated carrot
- 8 ounces (227 g) mushrooms, sliced
- ½ cup raisins
- 1 medium onion, chopped
- 1¼ cups chicken stock
- 2 garlic cloves, minced
- zest and juice of 1 lemon, juice
- 2 tbsps. olive oil
- ½ tsp. cumin
- ½ tsp. ground coriander

DIRECTIONS:
1. In a large wok over medium heat, heat the oil.
2. Add the onion, carrot and mushrooms and cook for 5 minutes.
3. Stir in the seasonings with lemon zest, couscous and raisins. Cook for about 2 minutes.
4. Stir in the lemon juice with chicken stock. Lower the heat and cook for about 3 to 4 minutes.
5. Cover the lid and turn off the heat. Allow it to sit for 5 to 6 minutes. Serve hot.

Alexandria Nutty Rice Casserole

Prep Time: 10 minutes, Cook Time: 30 minutes, Serves: 4

INGREDIENTS:
- 1½ ounces (43 g) pistachios, shelled
- 8 ounces (227 g) long-grain white rice
- 2.6 ounces (74 g) sultanas
- 1 small onion, sliced
- 1½ ounces (43 g) unsalted butter
- 2 small oranges, zested and juiced
- 4 garlic cloves, crushed
- 2½ cups chicken stock
- ½ tsp. turmeric
- 1 cinnamon stick
- 2 bay leaves
- A pinch of salt and black pepper

DIRECTIONS:
1. In a deep wok over medium heat, heat the butter. Add the garlic and onion and cook for 3 minutes.
2. Stir in the rice with cinnamon stick and cook for about 3 minutes.
3. Toss in the bay leaves with orange juice, orange zest, sultanas, a pinch of salt and pepper.
4. Mix the turmeric with stock. Then stir it into the rice pan. Cook until they start boiling.
5. Lower the heat and cover the lid. Cook for about 16 minutes.
6. Sprinkle with the pistachios and cook them for another 2 minutes. Serve your rice casserole hot.

Steamed Rice with Chinese Sausage and Bok Choy

Prep Time: 2 hours, Cook Time: 20 minutes, Serves: 4

INGREDIENTS:
- 1½ cups jasmine rice
- 4 baby bok choy heads, each sliced into 6 wedges
- 4 lap cheung (Chinese sausage) links or Spanish chorizo
- 1 small shallot, thinly sliced
- 1-inch fresh ginger piece, peeled and finely minced
- 1 garlic clove, peeled and finely minced
- ¼ cup vegetable oil
- 1 tbsp. dark soy sauce
- 2 tsps. light soy sauce
- 2 tsps. Shaoxing rice wine
- 1 tsp. sesame oil
- a pinch of ugar

DIRECTIONS:
1. In a mixing bowl, rinse the rice 3 or 4 times under cold water, swishing the rice around in the water to rinse off any starches. Use cold water to cover the rice and soak for 2 hours. Drain the rice through a fine-mesh sieve.
2. Carefully rinse two bamboo steamer baskets and their lids under cold water, then put one basket in the wok. Pour in 2 inches of water, or enough to make the water level reach above the bottom rim of the steamer by ¼ to ½ inch but not so high that the water surpasses the bottom of the steamer.
3. Line a plate with a piece of cheesecloth and arrange half the soaked rice to the plate. Place 2 sausages and half the bok choy on top, and loosely tie up the cheesecloth. Then there will be enough space around the rice so that it can expand. Put the plate in the steamer basket. Repeat the work with another plate, more cheesecloth, and the remaining sausages and bok choy in the second steamer basket, then stack it on top of the first and cover the lid.
4. Turn the heat to medium-high, and bring the water to a boil. Steam the rice for about 20 minutes, checking the water level frequently and adding more water as needed.
5. When the rice is steaming, heat the vegetable oil over medium heat in a small saucepan, until it just begins to smoke. Turn off the heat and place the ginger, shallot and garlic. Stir together and add the light soy sauce, dark soy sauce, rice wine, sesame oil and a pinch of sugar. Set aside to let rest.
6. When the rice is ready, carefully untie the cheesecloth and take the rice and bok choy to a platter. Cut the sausages diagonally and place on top of the rice. Serve hot with the ginger soy oil on the side.

Basmati Rice with Cashews

Prep Time: 30 minutes, Cook Time: 55 minutes, Serves: 6

INGREDIENTS:
- 1½ cups uncooked basmati rice, rinsed
- 1 medium onion, peeled and chopped
- 4 ounces (113 g) cashews
- 2 ounces (57 g) sultanas
- 2 cinnamon sticks
- 2 whole cloves
- 2 tbsps. vegetable oil
- 1 bay leaf
- 1 tsp. salt

DIRECTIONS:
1. Soak the rice in a large bowl of the water for 30 minutes.
2. Drain the rice well.
3. In a wok over medium-low heat, heat the oil and cook the onion until soft.
4. Place the remaining ingredients except the salt over medium heat and stir fry for 2 minutes.
5. Pour in 2 cups of the water with salt to the pan and bring to a boil.
6. Lower the heat and simmer, covered for 20 minutes.
7. Discard the cinnamon sticks, bay leaf and cloves and serve warm.

Mixed Nut Pilaf with Herbes

Prep Time: 30 minutes, Cook Time: 50 minutes, Serves: 4

INGREDIENTS:
- 1¼ cups basmati rice, rinsed
- ½ cup nuts (pistachios, cashews, slivered almonds)
- 1 onion, minced
- 2 garlic cloves, minced
- 2 cups chicken broth
- 2 tbsps. olive oil
- 1 tbsp. chopped cilantro
- 1 bay leaf
- 2 tsps. coriander powder
- 1 tsp. cumin seed
- ½ tsp. cardamom
- Salt and pepper

DIRECTIONS:
1. Soak the rice in a bowl of the fresh cold water for 30 minutes.
2. Drain the rice well.
3. In a larger wok over medium-high heat, heat the oil and cook the onion and garlic for 5 minutes.
4. Stir in the rice, bay leaf, cumin seeds, coriander and cardamom and cook for 2 minutes.
5. Toss in the broth, salt and pepper and bring to a boil.
6. Lower the heat and simmer, covered for 10 minutes.
7. Remove from heat and set aside, covered for 5 minutes.
8. Sprinkle with the nuts and toss to coat well.
9. Garnish with the cilantro and serve warm.

Shrimp Fried Rice with Peas

Prep Time: 15 minutes, Cook Time: 5 minutes, Serves: 4

INGREDIENTS:
- 2 cups cold, cooked rice
- ½ pound (227 g) medium shrimp, peeled, deveined, and halved lengthwise
- 1 cup frozen peas, thawed
- 2 large eggs, beaten
- 1 medium onion, diced
- 4 scallions, cut into ½-inch pieces
- 2 garlic cloves, crushed and chopped
- 2 tbsps. cooking oil
- 1 tbsp. ginger, crushed and chopped
- 1 tbsp. soy sauce
- 1 tsp. sesame oil
- ½ tsp. kosher salt

DIRECTIONS:
1. In a wok, heat the cooking oil over high heat until it shimmers.
2. Add the garlic, ginger, salt and eggs and stir-fry for about 1 minute, or until the eggs are firm.
3. Place the onion and shrimp and stir-fry for about 1 minute.
4. Toss the peas, sesame oil, rice and soy sauce and stir-fry for 1 minute.
5. Sprinkle with the scallions and serve hot.

Indonesian Tomato Egg Fried Rice

Prep Time: 15 minutes, Cook Time: 8 minutes, Serves: 4

INGREDIENTS:
- 2 cups cold, cooked rice
- 4 eggs
- 2 tomatoes, sliced
- ½ pound (227 g) ground meat of your choice
- 1 cucumber, sliced
- 1 medium onion, diced
- 4 scallions, cut into ½-inch pieces
- 2 garlic cloves, crushed and chopped
- ¼ cup kecap manis
- 3 tbsps. cooking oil, divided
- 1 tbsp. ginger, crushed and chopped
- 1 tsp. hot sesame oil

DIRECTIONS:
1. In a wok, heat 2 tbsps. of the cooking oil over high heat until it shimmers.
2. Add the meat, garlic, ginger and onion and stir-fry for about 1 minute.
3. Place the rice, sesame oil, kecap manis and scallions and stir-fry for 1 minute. Transfer to a serving bowl.
4. Pour the remaining 1 tbsp. of cooking oil to the wok and, once the oil is shimmering, fry the eggs sunny-side up.
5. Put a fried egg on top of rice, and sliced tomatoes and cucumbers on the side. Serve warm.

Chapter 5 Grain and Rice

Chinese Sausage Fried Rice with Peas

Prep Time: 15 minutes, Cook Time: 8 minutes, Serves: 4

INGREDIENTS:
2 links cured Chinese sausage, sliced into ½-inch pieces
2 large eggs, beaten
2 cups cold, cooked rice
1 cup frozen peas, thawed
4 scallions, cut into ½-inch pieces
2 garlic cloves, crushed and chopped
2 tbsps. soy sauce
1 tbsp. cooking oil
1 tbsp. ginger, crushed and chopped
1 tbsp. sesame oil

DIRECTIONS:
1. In a wok, heat the cooking oil over high heat until it shimmers.
2. Add the garlic, ginger and sausage and stir-fry for about 1 minute.
3. Push the sausage to the sides of the wok, then add the eggs and stir-fry for about 1 minute.
4. Put the peas, rice, soy sauce and sesame oil and stir-fry for 1 minute.
5. Garnish with the scallions and serve warm.

Fried Rice with Smoked Trout

Prep Time: 10 minutes, Cook Time: 10 minutes, Serves: 4

INGREDIENTS:
3 cups cold cooked rice
4 ounces (113 g) smoked trout, broken into bite-size pieces
2 large eggs
½ cup thinly sliced hearts of romaine lettuce
2 scallions, thinly sliced
2 garlic cloves, finely minced
3 tbsps. ghee or vegetable oil, divided
1 tbsp. light soy sauce
1 tsp. sesame oil
1 tsp. peeled finely minced fresh ginger
½ tsp. sugar
½ tsp. white sesame seeds
Kosher salt
Ground white pepper

DIRECTIONS:
1. Whisk the eggs with the sesame oil and a pinch each of salt and white pepper in a large bowl, until just combined. Stir the light soy and sugar together to dissolve the sugar entirely in a small bowl. Set aside.
2. Heat a wok over high heat until a drop of water sizzles and evaporates on contact. Add 1 tbsp. of ghee and swirl to coat the base of the wok well. Pour in the egg mixture and swirl and shake the eggs with a heatproof spatula to cook. Take the eggs to a plate when just cooked but not dry.
3. Pour in the remaining 2 tbsps. of ghee to the wok, along with the ginger and garlic. Stir-fry immediately until the garlic and ginger just are fragrant, but take care not to let them burn. Place the rice and soy mixture and stir to combine well. Continue stir-frying, for about 3 minutes. Put the trout and cooked egg and stir-fry to break them up, for about 20 seconds. Then arrange the lettuce and scallions and stir-fry until they are both bright green.
4. Remove from the heat and sprinkle with the sesame seeds. Serve warm.

Fried Rice with Shrimp and Egg

Prep Time: 10 minutes, Cook Time: 10 minutes, Serves: 4

INGREDIENTS:
1 large egg, beaten
½ pound (227 g) shrimp (any size), peeled, deveined, and cut into bite-size pieces
2 garlic cloves, finely minced
½ cup frozen peas and carrots
2 scallions, thinly sliced, divided
3 cups cold cooked rice
3 tbsps. unsalted butter
2 tbsps. vegetable oil
1 tbsp. light soy sauce
1 tbsp. sesame oil
1 tsp. peeled finely minced fresh ginger
Kosher salt

DIRECTIONS:
1. Heat a wok over high heat until a drop of water sizzles and evaporates on contact. Add the vegetable oil and swirl to coat the base of the wok well. Season the oil with a small pinch of salt. Place the egg and scramble quickly.
2. Push the egg to the sides of the wok to create a center ring, then put the shrimp, ginger and garlic together. Stir-fry the shrimp with a small pinch of salt for about 2 to 3 minutes, until they turn opaque and pink. Place the peas and carrots and half the scallions and stir-fry for 1 more minute.
3. Add the rice, breaking up any large lumps, and sitr and flip to combine all of the ingredients. Stir-fry for about 1 minute, then push it all to the sides of the wok, creating a well in the bottom of the wok.
4. Pour in the butter and light soy, allow the butter to melt and bubble, then toss everything together to coat well, about 30 seconds.
5. Arrange the fried rice evenly in the wok and let the rice sit against the wok for about 2 minutes to crisp up slightly. Drizzle with sesame oil and season with a small pinch of salt. Remove from the heat and serve hot, garnishing with the rest of the scallions.

Simple Sinangag

Prep Time: 15 minutes, Cook Time: 6 minutes, Serves: 4

INGREDIENTS:

2 cups cold, cooked rice
8 cloves garlic, crushed and chopped
4 scallions, cut into ¼-inch pieces
2 tbsps. cooking oil
¼ tsp. kosher salt

DIRECTIONS:

1. In a wok, heat the cooking oil and garlic over medium-high heat. Stir-fry for about 2 minutes until the garlic becomes golden brown but does not burn.
2. Take half the garlic and reserve it for garnishing.
3. Slowly sprinkle the rice and salt into the wok and stir-fry for about 1 minute.
4. Garnish with the chopped scallions and caramelized garlic. Serve warm.

Kimchi Fried Rice with Mushroom

Prep Time: 15 minutes, Cook Time: 8 minutes, Serves: 4

INGREDIENTS:

½ pound (227 g) thick-sliced bacon, cut into 1-inch pieces
2 cups cold, cooked rice
1 cup kimchi, cut into ½-inch pieces
4 ounces (113 g) sliced mushrooms
4 large eggs
4 scallions, cut into ½-inch pieces
2 garlic cloves, crushed and chopped
¼ cup kimchi juice
1 tbsp. ginger, crushed and chopped
1 tbsp. soy sauce
1 tsp. sesame oil

DIRECTIONS:

1. In a wok over high heat, place the bacon, ginger and garlic and stir-fry for 2 minutes, or until the bacon is lightly browned.
2. Drain off all but 2 tbsps. of the bacon fat from the wok and let rest.
3. Add the mushrooms to the wok and stir-fry for about 1 minute.
4. Place the kimchi and stir-fry for 30 seconds.
5. Toss in the rice, sesame oil, soy sauce, scallions and kimchi juice. Stir-fry for about 30 seconds, then transfer to a serving dish.
6. Take 2 tbsps. of the reserved bacon fat back to the wok and fry the eggs sunny-side up.
7. Top the fried eggs over the rice and serve.

Vegetable Egg Fried Rice

Prep Time: 15 minutes, Cook Time: 8 minutes, Serves: 4

INGREDIENTS:

4 large eggs, beaten
2 cups cold, cooked rice
1 cup frozen peas, thawed
1 medium carrot, julienned
1 medium onion, diced
1 red bell pepper, diced
4 scallions, cut into ½-inch pieces
2 garlic cloves, crushed and chopped
2 tbsps. cooking oil
1 tbsp. soy sauce
1 tbsp. ginger, crushed and chopped
1 tsp. sesame oil
½ tsp. kosher salt

DIRECTIONS:

1. In a wok, heat the cooking oil over high heat until it shimmers.
2. Add the garlic, ginger, salt and eggs and stir-fry for about 1 minute, or until the eggs are firm.
3. Place the onion, carrot and bell pepper and stir-fry for 1 minute.
4. Toss in the peas, rice, sesame oil, and soy sauce and stir-fry for 1 minute.
5. Top with the scallions and serve hot.

Chicken Chow Mein with Bok Choy, page 32

Beef Lo Mein with Bean Sprouts, page 31

Sesame Noodles with Peanut Butter, page 30

Egg Noodles with Scallions, page 31

Chapter 6 Pasta

Chapter 6 Pasta

Honey Chow Mein with Vegetable

Prep Time: 15 minutes, Cook Time: 6 minutes, Serves: 4

INGREDIENTS:
- 1 pound (454 g) cooked noodles
- 2 cups sugar snap or snow pea pods
- 1 medium onion, cut into 1-inch pieces
- 1 red bell pepper, cut into 1-inch pieces
- 4 scallions, cut into 1-inch pieces
- 2 garlic cloves, crushed and chopped
- ¼ cup cooking oil
- ¼ cup hoisin sauce
- 2 tbsps. honey
- 2 tbsps. soy sauce
- 2 tbsps. Shaoxing rice wine
- 1 tbsp. ginger, crushed and chopped

DIRECTIONS:
1. In a wok, heat the cooking oil over high heat until it shimmers.
2. Add the noodles and stir-fry for about 2 minutes until lightly browned.
3. Take the noodles and drain off all but 2 tbsps. of oil.
4. Place the garlic, ginger and onion to the wok and stir-fry for 1 minute.
5. Put the bell pepper and pea pods and stir-fry for 1 minute.
6. Toss the noodles, honey, hoisin sauce, soy sauce and rice wine and stir-fry for 1 minute.
7. Sprinkle with the scallions and serve warm.

Cold Scallion Noodles

Prep Time: 10 minutes, Cook Time: 15 minutes, Serves: 6 to 8

INGREDIENTS:
- 6 ounces (170 g) whole-grain spaghetti
- 1 carrot, julienned
- 1-inch piece ginger, peeled and minced
- 2 scallions, chopped
- 2 tbsps. sesame oil, divided
- 2 tbsps. soy sauce
- 1 tbsp. sesame seeds
- 1 tbsp. rice vinegar
- 2 tsps. brown sugar or honey
- 2 tsps. peanut butter

DIRECTIONS:
1. Carefully cook the spaghetti according to the package directions for al dente. Rinse the noodles with cold water and drizzle in 1 tbsp. of sesame oil to prevent the noodles from sticking.
2. Combine the remaining 1 tbsp. of sesame oil, the soy sauce, vinegar, brown sugar, and peanut butter in a small bowl, mixing well.
3. Add the mixture over the noodles then place the carrot, ginger, scallions, and sesame seeds, tossing to combine well.
4. Serve chilled.

Fried Vermicelli Noodles with Mushrooms

Prep Time: 35 minutes, Cook Time: 10 minutes, Serves: 4

INGREDIENTS:
- 4 to 6 large dried shiitake mushrooms
- Water for soaking noodles and mushrooms
- 1 (8-ounce / 227-g) package dried rice vermicelli noodles
- **SAUCE:**
- ¼ cup soy sauce
- 1 tsp. dark soy sauce
- 2 pinches ground white pepper
- ½ tsp. sugar
- 2 tbsps. water
- **STIR-FRY:**
- 2 tbsps. peanut oil
- 2 cups fresh mung bean sprouts, rinsed
- 2 cups shredded cabbage
- 2 garlic cloves, minced
- 2 scallions, cut into 1-inch pieces

DIRECTIONS:
1. Soak the noodles with warm water in a large bowl. Then soak the shiitake mushrooms with hot water in a small bowl. Let the noodles and the mushrooms soften for about 30 minutes.
2. Drain the noodles through a colander, and set them aside.
3. Slice the mushrooms into thin strips.
4. Prepare the sauce by mixing together the soy sauce, water, dark soy sauce, sugar, and pepper in a small bowl. Set it aside.
5. In a wok, heat the peanut oil over medium-high heat.
6. Add the garlic and stir-fry until fragrant, for 20 seconds.
7. Stir in the cabbage and stir-fry until slightly wilted.
8. Place the vermicelli noodles and the sauce. Stir-fry for 5 minutes, until the noodles have absorbed all the liquid entirely.
9. Put the bean sprouts and scallions, and stir-fry just to combine them into the noodles.
10. Transfer the noodles to a serving plate and serve hot.

Rice Noodles with Beef and Broccoli

Prep Time: 20 minutes, Cook Time: 10 minutes, Serves: 4

INGREDIENTS:

1½ pounds (680 g) fresh wide rice noodles or dried rice noodles
¾ pound (340 g) flank steak or sirloin tips, sliced across the grain into ⅛-inch-thick slices
1 bunch Chinese broccoli (gai lan), stems sliced diagonally into ½-inch pieces, leaves cut into bite-size pieces
2 large eggs, beaten
4 garlic cloves, thinly sliced
5 tbsps. vegetable oil, divided
2 tbsps. oyster sauce
1 tbsp. light soy sauce
2 tsps. dark soy sauce
2 tsps. cornstarch
2 tsps. fish sauce, divided
½ tsp. sugar
½ tsp. kosher salt
Ground white pepper

DIRECTIONS:

1. Stir together the dark soy, cornstarch, 1 tsp. of fish sauce, salt and a pinch of white pepper in a mixing bowl. Add the beef slices and toss to coat well. Set aside to marinate for about 10 minutes.
2. Stir together the oyster sauce, light soy, remaining 1 tsp. of fish sauce and sugar in another bowl. Set aside.
3. If using fresh rice noodles, rinse them with hot water to keep them separated, and set aside. If using dried rice noodles, cook them according to the package instructions, drain and set aside.
4. Heat a wok over high heat until a drop of water sizzles and evaporates on contact. Add 2 tbsps. of oil and swirl to coat the base of the wok evenly. Transfer the beef to the wok with tongs and reserve the marinade. Sear the beef against the wok for about 2 to 3 minutes, until it's brown and a seared crust develops. Take the beef back to the marinade bowl and stir in the oyster sauce mixture.
5. Pour in 2 more tbsps. of oil and stir-fry the garlic for about 30 seconds. Place the Chinese broccoli stems and stir-fry for about 45 seconds, keeping moving frequently to prevent the garlic from burning.
6. Push the broccoli stems to the sides of the wok, making the bottom of the wok empty. Add the remaining 1 tbsp. of oil and scramble the eggs in the well, then toss them together.
7. Put the noodles, sauce and beef, and toss and flip immediately to combine all of the ingredients, stir-frying for 30 more seconds. Place the broccoli leaves and stir-fry for 30 seconds more, or until the leaves are wilted. Transfer to a platter and serve hot.

Singapore Noodles with Shrimp

Prep Time: 10 minutes, Cook Time: 20 minutes, Serves: 4

INGREDIENTS:

½ pound (227 g) dried rice vermicelli noodles
½ pound (227 g) medium shrimp, peeled and deveined
½ pound (227 g) char shiu (Chinese roast pork), sliced into thin strips
1 cup frozen peas, thawed
1 small white onion, thinly sliced into strips
½ green bell pepper, cut into thin strips
½ red bell pepper, cut into thin strips
8 to 10 fresh cilantro sprigs
2 garlic cloves, finely minced
Juice of 1 lime
3 tbsps. coconut oil, divided
2 tsps. curry powder
1 tsp. fish sauce (optional)
Kosher salt
Freshly ground black pepper

DIRECTIONS:

1. Bring a large pot of water to boil over medium-high heat. Turn off the heat and place the noodles. Soak for about 4 to 5 minutes, until the noodles become opaque. Gently drain the noodles in a colander. Rinse the noodles under cold water and set aside.
2. Season the shrimp with the fish sauce (if using) in a small bowl, and set aside for 5 minutes. If you don't want to use fish sauce, use a pinch of salt to season the shrimp instead.
3. Heat a wok over high heat until a drop of water sizzles and evaporates on contact. Add 2 tbsps. of coconut oil and swirl to coat the base of the wok well. Season the oil with a small pinch of salt. Put the shrimp and stir-fry for about 3 to 4 minutes, or until the shrimp is pink. Remove to a clean bowl and set aside.
4. Pour in the remaining 1 tbsp. of coconut oil and swirl to coat the wok evenly. Stir-fry the bell peppers, onion, and garlic for 3 to 4 minutes, until the onions and peppers are tender. Add the peas and stir-fry until just heated through, about another 1 minute.
5. Arrange the pork and return the shrimp to the wok. Stir together with the curry powder, salt and pepper. Place the noodles and toss to combine well. As you continue to gently toss them with the other ingredients, the noodles will turn a brilliant golden yellow color. Continue stir-frying and tossing for 2 minutes, until the noodles are heated through.
6. Take the noodles to a platter, drizzle with the lime juice, and sprinkle with the cilantro. Serve hot.

Asian Spicy Pasta with Tomatoes

Prep Time: 20 minutes, Cook Time: 10 minutes, Serves: 4

INGREDIENTS:

1 cup pasta to pick as per your liking
3 tomatoes, thinly diced
1 onion, tiny sliced
3 garlic cloves, sliced
1 cup water or, as needed
1 tbsp. olive oil
1 tbsp. powder of turmeric
1 tbsp. powder of coriander
1 tsp. seed cumin
1 tsp. option curry powder
Ground red chili as per your taste
Salt as per your taste

DIRECTIONS:

1. Heat oil in a wok over medium-high heat. Let it get warm.
2. Add onions, garlic, and cumin seed and cook for a while.
3. Place the tomatoes, all the dried spices and salt and cook them until they are soft, for 1 or 2 minutes.
4. Pour in the pasta and water. Mix well then turn off stir fry mode.
5. Cover the lid and let it cook for 20 minutes.
6. Serve hot.

Hakka Noodles with Pork and Cabbage

Prep Time: 15 minutes, Cook Time: 6 minutes, Serves: 4

INGREDIENTS:

1 pound (454 g) cooked noodles
1 pound (454 g) ground pork
1 medium carrot, julienned
1 medium onion, diced
1 cup shredded cabbage
2 garlic cloves, crushed and chopped
1 scallion, cut into ½-inch pieces
2 tbsps. cooking oil
1 tbsp. ginger, crushed and chopped
1 tbsp. fish sauce
1 tbsp. soy sauce
1 tbsp. hoisin sauce
1 tsp. hot sesame oil
1 tsp. ground coriander

DIRECTIONS:

1. In a wok, heat the oil over high heat until it shimmers.
2. Add the garlic, ginger and pork and stir-fry for 1 minute.
3. Place the onion, carrot and cabbage and stir-fry for 1 minute.
4. Put the noodles and stir-fry for 1 minute.
5. Toss the soy sauce, fish sauce, hoisin, coriander and sesame oil and stir-fry for 1 minute.
6. Garnish with the scallion and serve warm.

Chinese Birthday Noodles with Shrimp

Prep Time: 10 minutes, Cook Time: 10 minutes, Serves: 4

INGREDIENTS:

¾ pound (340 g) egg noodles
½ pound (227 g) medium shrimp, peeled and deveined
4 ounces (113 g) char shiu (Chinese barbecue pork), sliced into thin strips
6 to 8 fresh shiitake mushrooms, stems removed and caps thinly sliced
½ cup frozen edamame beans, shelled and thawed
4 scallions, trimmed, white and green parts thinly sliced
1 shallot, thinly sliced
3 tbsps. sesame oil, divided
3 tbsps. coarsely chopped fresh cilantro
2 tbsps. vegetable oil
1 tbsp. light soy sauce
2 tsps. Shaoxing rice wine
Kosher salt

DIRECTIONS:

1. Bring a pot of water to a boil over high heat and cook the noodles according to package instructions. Drain and rinse the noodles with cold water. Drizzle 1 tbsp. of sesame oil over the noodles and set aside.
2. Heat a wok over high heat until a drop of water sizzles and evaporates on contact. Add the vegetable oil and swirl to coat the base of the wok well. Place the mushrooms and toss to coat with the oil evenly. Allow the mushrooms to sit against the wok and sear for about 1 to 2 minutes. Toss and flip the mushrooms around for 30 seconds more, or until golden brown.
3. Put the shrimp and shallot and toss with the mushrooms. Stir-fry for about 2 to 3 minutes, until the shrimp becomes opaque and pink. Season with a small pinch of salt. Arrange the char shui and edamame, tossing and flipping until heated through, about 1 minute. Pour in the light soy and rice wine and toss to coat well.
4. Sprinkle with the scallions and cilantro, reserving a small bit of each for garnish, and toss until the cilantro is wilted slightly. Place the noodles and another pinch of salt. Toss and scoop, lifting upward to separate the noodle strands and combine with the shrimp and vegetables.
5. Remove from the heat and drizzle with the remaining 2 tbsps. of sesame oil. Garnish with the reserved scallions and cilantro. Serve warm.

Tasty Beef Chow Fun

Prep Time: 15 minutes, Cook Time: 10 minutes, Serves: 4

INGREDIENTS:

¾ pound (340 g) flank steak or sirloin tips, cut across the grain into ⅛-inch-thick slices
1½ pounds (680 g) fresh wide rice noodles or ¾ pound (340 g) dried
2 cups fresh mung bean sprouts
4 peeled fresh ginger slices, each about the size of a quarter
8 scallions, halved lengthwise and cut into 3-inch pieces
¼ cup Shaoxing rice wine
¼ cup light soy sauce
3 tbsps. vegetable oil, divided
2 tbsps. cornstarch
2 tbsps. sesame oil, divided
1½ tbsps. dark soy sauce
½ tsp. sugar
Kosher salt
Ground white pepper

DIRECTIONS:

1. Stir together the rice wine, light soy, cornstarch, dark soy, sugar, and a pinch of white pepper in a mixing bowl. Place the beef and toss to coat well. Set aside to marinate for at least 10 minutes.
2. Bring a large pot of water to a boil over high heat and cook the rice noodles according to package instructions. Reserve 1 cup of the cooking water and drain the the noodles. Rinse under cold water and drizzle in 1 tbsp. of sesame oil. Set aside.
3. Heat a wok over high heat until a drop of water sizzles and evaporates on contact. Add 2 tbsps. of vegetable oil and swirl to coat the base of the wok well. Season the oil with the ginger and a pinch of salt. Let the ginger sizzle in the oil for about 30 seconds, swirling slowly.
4. Arrange the beef to the wok with tongs, and reserve the marinating liquid. Sear the beef against the wok for about 2 to 3 minutes, or until a seared, browned crust develops. Constantly toss and flip the beef around the wok for 1 more minute. Transfer the beef to a clean bowl and set aside.
5. Drizzle in 1 more tbsp. of vegetable oil and stir-fry the scallions for about 30 seconds, or until tender. Put the noodles and lift in a scooping upward motion to help separate the noodles if they have stuck together. Pour in the cooking water, 1 tbsp. at a time, if the noodles have really glued themselves together.
6. Take the beef back to the wok and toss to combine with the noodles. Add the reserved marinade and toss for about 30 seconds to 1 minute, or until the sauce thickens and coats the noodles well and they turn a deep, rich brown color. If necessary, pour in 1 tbsp. of the reserved cooking water to thin out the sauce. Place the bean sprouts and toss until just heated through, about 1 minute. Scoop out the ginger and discard.
7. Transfer the noodles to a platter and drizzle with the remaining 1 tbsp. of sesame oil. Serve warm.

Sesame Noodles with Peanut Butter

Prep Time: 15 minutes, Cook Time: 5 minutes, Serves: 4

INGREDIENTS:

1 pound (454 g) cooked noodles
4 scallions, cut into ½-inch pieces
2 garlic cloves, crushed and chopped
¼ cup peanut butter
¼ cup peanut oil
2 tbsps. cooking oil
2 tbsps. powdered sugar
2 tbsps. soy sauce
1 tbsp. sesame seeds
1 tbsp. hot sesame oil
1 tbsp. ginger, crushed and chopped

DIRECTIONS:

1. Whisk together the peanut butter, peanut oil, sesame oil, powdered sugar and soy sauce until smooth in a medium bowl. Set aside.
2. In a wok, heat the cooking oil over high heat until it shimmers.
3. Add the garlic, ginger and noodles and stir-fry for about 1 minute.
4. Pour in the peanut butter mixture and toss for about 30 seconds.
5. Sprinkle with the scallions and sesame seeds and serve warm.

Seafood Lo Mein with Pork

Prep Time: 15 minutes, Cook Time: 6 minutes, Serves: 4

INGREDIENTS:

1 pound (454 g) cooked noodles
¼ pound (113 g) medium shrimp, peeled, deveined, and cut in half lengthwise
¼ pound (113 g) sea scallops, cut in half widthwise
¼ pound (113 g) ground pork
1 medium onion, cut into 1-inch pieces
1 red bell pepper, cut into 1-inch pieces
¼ cup oyster sauce
2 garlic cloves, crushed and chopped
2 tbsps. soy sauce
2 tbsps. rice wine
2 tbsps. cooking oil
1 tbsp. ginger, crushed and chopped

DIRECTIONS:

1. In a wok, heat the cooking oil over high heat until it

shimmers.
2. Add the garlic, ginger, pork, and onion and stir-fry for about 1 minute.
3. Place the bell pepper and shrimp and stir-fry for about 1 minute.
4. Put the scallops and stir-fry for about 30 seconds.
5. Whisk together the soy sauce, rice wine and oyster sauce in a small bowl, then pour the mixture to the wok.
6. Toss in the noodles and stir-fry for 30 seconds.
7. Serve hot.

Beef Lo Mein with Bean Sprouts

Prep Time: 15 minutes, Cook Time: 20 minutes, Serves: 4

INGREDIENTS:

½ pound (227 g) fresh lo mein egg noodles
½ pound (227 g) beef sirloin tips, sliced across the grain into thin strips
2 cups mung bean sprouts
1 cup snow peas, strings removed
½ red bell pepper, sliced into thin strips
2 garlic cloves, finely minced
2 peeled fresh ginger slices, each about the size of a quarter
3 tbsps. vegetable oil, divided
2 tbsps. sesame oil, divided
2 tbsps. Shaoxing rice wine
2 tbsps. cornstarch, divided
2 tbsps. dark soy sauce
Kosher salt
Ground white pepper

DIRECTIONS:

1. Bring a pot of water to a boil over high heat and cook the noodles according to package instructions. Reserve ¼ cup of the cooking water and drain the noodles through a colander. Rinse the noodles with cold water and drain excess water again. Drizzle 1 tbsp. of sesame oil over noodles and toss to coat well. Set aside.
2. Stir together the rice wine, 2 tsps. of cornstarch, dark soy, and a generous pinch of white pepper in a mixing bowl. Place the beef and toss to coat. Set aside for about 10 minutes to marinate.
3. Heat a wok over high heat until a drop of water sizzles and evaporates on contact. Add the vegetable oil and swirl to coat the base of the wok well. Season the oil with the ginger and a small pinch of salt. Let the ginger sizzle in the oil for 30 seconds, swirling slowly. Place the beef, reserving the marinade, and sear against the wok for about 2 to 3 minutes. Toss and flip the beef constantly, stir-frying for 1 more minute, or until no longer pink. Take to a bowl and set aside.
4. Pour in the remaining 1 tbsp. of vegetable oil and stir-fry the bell pepper, tossing and flipping for about 2 to 3 minutes, until soft. Put the snow peas and garlic, stir-frying for another minute, or until the garlic is aromatic.
5. Push all the ingredients to the sides of the wok and add the remaining 1 tbsp. of sesame oil, remaining 4 tsps. of cornstarch, reserved marinade, and ¼ cup of the reserved cooking water. Toss together and bring to a boil. Take the beef back to the wok and toss to combine with the vegetables for about 1 to 2 minutes, until the sauce turns thick and glossy.
6. Stir in the lo mein noodles with the beef and vegetables until the noodles are evenly coated with the sauce. Add the bean sprouts and toss to combine well. Scoop out and discard the ginger. Take the noodles to a platter and serve hot.

Egg Noodles with Scallions

Prep Time: 10 minutes, Cook Time: 10 minutes, Serves: 4

INGREDIENTS:

½ pound (227 g) fresh Chinese egg noodles
8 garlic cloves, finely minced
6 scallions, thinly sliced
6 tbsps. unsalted butter
2 tbsps. sesame oil, divided
2 tbsps. oyster sauce
2 tbsps. light brown sugar
1 tbsp. light soy sauce
½ tsps. ground white pepper

DIRECTIONS:

1. Bring a pot of water to a boil over high heat and cook the egg noodles according to package directions. Reserve 1 cup of the boiling water, then drain. Drizzle 1 tbsp. of sesame oil over the noodles and toss to coat well. Set aside.
2. Stir together the brown sugar, oyster sauce, light soy and white pepper in a small bowl. Set aside.
3. In a wok over medium-high heat, melt the butter until the foaming stops. Add the minced garlic and half the scallions. Stir-fry for about 30 seconds, or until the garlic is softened.
4. Pour in the sauce and toss to combine with the butter and garlic. Bring the sauce to a simmer and place the noodles. Toss the noodles to coat with sauce evenly. If the noodles need to loosen up a bit, pour in some of the cooking water, 1 tbsp. at a time. Continue to stir-fry the noodles for about 2 to 3 minutes, until they are heated completely.
5. Remove the noodles to a platter and garnish with the remaining scallions. Serve warm.

Chicken Chow Mein with Bok Choy

Prep Time: 15 minutes, Cook Time: 15 minutes, Serves: 4

INGREDIENTS:

½ pound (227 g) fresh thin Hong Kong–style egg noodles
½ pound (227 g) chicken thighs, sliced into thin strips
3 heads baby bok choy, cut into bite-sized pieces
1 large handful (2 to 3 ounces / 57 to 85 g) mung bean sprouts
2 garlic cloves, finely minced
¼ cup low-sodium chicken broth
4 tbsps. vegetable oil, divided
1½ tbsps. sesame oil, divided
2 tsps. cornstarch
2 tsps. dark soy sauce
2 tsps. oyster sauce
2 tsps. Shaoxing rice wine
2 tsps. light soy sauce
Ground white pepper

DIRECTIONS:

1. Bring a pot of water to a boil over high heat and cook the noodles according to package instructions. Reserve 1 cup of the cooking water and drain the noodles through a colander. Rinse the noodles under cold water and pour in 1 tbsp. of sesame oil. Toss to coat well and set aside.
2. Combine the rice wine, light soy and a pinch of white pepper in a mixing bowl. Toss the chicken pieces to coat and marinate for about 10 minutes. Stir together the chicken broth, dark soy, remaining ½ tbsp. of sesame oil, oyster sauce, and cornstarch in a small bowl. Set aside.
3. Heat a wok over high heat until a drop of water sizzles and evaporates on contact. Add 3 tbsps. of vegetable oil and swirl to coat the base of the wok well. Arrange the noodles in one layer and fry for about 2 to 3 minutes, or until they are golden brown. Flip the noodles over gently and fry on the other side for another 2 minutes, or until the noodles are crispy and brown, and have formed into a loose cake. Take the noodles to a paper towel–lined plate and set aside.
4. Pour in the remaining 1 tbsp. of vegetable oil and stir-fry the chicken and marinade for about 2 to 3 minutes, until the chicken is no longer pink and the marinade has evaporated. Place the bok choy and garlic, stir-frying until the bok choy stems are soft, about 1 minute.
5. Add the sauce and stir to combine with the chicken and bok choy.
6. Return the noodles and toss the noodles with the chicken and vegetables for about 2 minutes, until coated evenly with the sauce. If the noodles are a bit dry, pour in a tbsp. or so of the reserved cooking water as you toss. Place the bean sprouts and stir-fry, lifting and scooping for 1 more minute.
7. Remove from the heat and serve hot.

Canton Pancit

Prep Time: 15 minutes, Cook Time: 8 minutes, Serves: 4

INGREDIENTS:

1 pound (454 g) cooked Hong Kong–style noodles
¼ pound (113 g) boneless chicken thighs, cut into 1-inch pieces
¼ pound (113 g) thinly sliced sirloin steak, cut into 1-inch pieces
¼ pound (113 g) medium shrimp, peeled, deveined, and cut in half lengthwise
1 medium onion, cut into 1-inch pieces
1 medium carrot, julienned
4 ounces (113 g) shiitake mushrooms, sliced
¼ cup oyster sauce
¼ cup meat or vegetable broth
4 scallions, cut into 1-inch pieces
Lemon wedges
2 garlic cloves, crushed and chopped
2 tbsps. cooking oil
2 tbsps. soy sauce
1 tbsp. ginger, crushed and chopped
1 tbsp. fish sauce

DIRECTIONS:

1. In a wok, heat the oil over high heat until it shimmers.
2. Add the garlic, ginger, chicken and carrot and stir-fry for 1 minute.
3. Place the steak, mushrooms and onion and stir-fry for 1 minute.
4. Toss the shrimp, soy sauce, fish sauce, oyster sauce, and broth and stir-fry for 1 minute.
5. Add the noodles and stir-fry for 1 minute.
6. Sprinkle with the scallions and serve with the lemon wedges.

Chinese Steamed Fish, page 38

Simple Ginger and Scallion Crab, page 38

Fried Chips and Cod Fish, page 34

Mussels with Tomato Sauce, page 41

Chapter 7 Fish and Seafood 33

Chapter 7 Fish and Seafood

Curried Shrimp with Basmati

Prep Time: 25 minutes, Cook Time: 20 minutes, Serves: 5

INGREDIENTS:
1 pound (454 g) large shrimp, peeled and deveined
1 cup tomato juice
½ cup heavy cream
Cooked basmati rice
1 small onion, diced
2 stalks celery, strings removed, diced
2 oranges, zest and juice
2 tbsps. olive oil
1 tbsp. hot curry powder
1 tsp. dried oregano
Coarse salt
Ground black pepper

DIRECTIONS:
1. Mix together the shrimp, half of the orange zest, 1½ tsps. of the curry powder, ¼ tsp. of the salt and ¼ tsp. of the pepper in a large bowl.
2. In a large wok over medium heat, heat 1 tbsp. of the oil and cook the shrimp for 2 minutes per side.
3. Transfer the shrimp to a plate.
4. In the same wok, heat the remaining oil and cook the onion, celery, dried oregano and remaining 1½ tsps. of the curry powder for 4 minutes.
5. Toss in the orange and tomato juices and cook for 8 minutes.
6. Place the cooked shrimp and cook for 2 minutes.
7. Stir in the remaining orange zest, cream, salt and pepper and turn off the heat.
8. Serve over cooked basmati rice.

Fried Chips and Cod Fish

Prep Time: 10 minutes, Cook Time: 35 minutes, Serves: 4

INGREDIENTS:
1½ pounds (680 g) cod fillets
4 large potatoes, peeled and cut into strips lengthwise
1 cup all-purpose flour
1 egg, beaten lightly
4 cups vegetable oil
1 cup milk
1 tsp. baking powder
Salt and freshly ground black pepper, to taste

DIRECTIONS:
1. Add flour, baking powder, salt, black pepper, egg and milk in a large bowl.
2. Mix until well combined.
3. Set aside for at least 20 minutes.
4. Dip the potatoes in a large bowl of chilled water, for 2 to 3 minutes.
5. Drain the potatoes well and pat dry with paper towel.
6. In a large wok over medium heat, heat the oil.
7. Place the potatoes and fry for 3 to 4 minutes or until crisp and tender.
8. Gently transfer the potatoes onto a paper towel lined plate.
9. Coat the cod fillets in the flour mixture evenly.
10. Fry the cod fillets for about 3 to 4 minutes or till golden brown.
11. Take the cod fillets onto another paper towel lined plate.
12. Now, take the potato strips back to the wok and fry them for 1 to 2 minutes more or till crispy. Serve hot.

Ginger Mussels in Black Bean Sauce

Prep Time: 5 minutes, Cook Time: 5 minutes, Serves: 4 to 6

INGREDIENTS:
SAUCE:
1 cup water
1 tbsp. black bean sauce
1 tsp. soy sauce
1 tsp. rice vinegar
½ tsp. dark soy sauce
1 tsp. sugar
STIR-FRY:
2 pounds (907 g) fresh mussels, scrubbed and debearded
2-inch piece ginger, peeled and julienned
2 garlic cloves, minced
1 scallion, chopped into 1-inch pieces
1 tbsp. peanut oil
1 tsp. sesame oil

DIRECTIONS:
1. Prepare the sauce by combining the water, black bean sauce, rice vinegar, sugar, soy sauce, and dark soy sauce in a small bowl. Set it aside.
2. In a wok, heat the peanut oil over medium-high heat.
3. Place the ginger and garlic and stir-fry for 20 seconds or until aromatic.
4. Pour in the mussels and sauce. Stir and lower the heat.
5. Cover the lid for 5 minutes, uncovering to stir the mussels every minute or so.
6. When most of the shells have opened, remove from the heat and add the sesame oil and scallions. Throw any unopened mussels away.
7. Transfer the mussels to a serving dish and serve hot.

Shrimp and Pork with Lobster Sauce

Prep Time: 15 minutes, Cook Time: 8 minutes, Serves: 4

INGREDIENTS:
½ pound (227 g) medium shrimp, peeled and deveined
½ pound (227 g) ground pork
2 large eggs, beaten
½ cup thawed frozen peas
4 scallions, cut into ½-inch pieces
3 garlic cloves, crushed and chopped
1 cup chicken stock
2 tbsps. cooking oil
2 tbsps. cornstarch
2 tbsps. soy sauce
1 tbsp. ginger, crushed and chopped
1 tbsp. rice wine
1 tsp. hot sesame oil
1 tsp. sugar

DIRECTIONS:
1. Whisk together the stock, cornstarch, soy sauce, sesame oil, and sugar in a small bowl. Set aside.
2. In a wok, heat the cooking oil over high heat until it shimmers.
3. Add the ginger and garlic and stir-fry for 1 minute.
4. Place the pork, shrimp and rice wine and stir-fry for about 1 minute.
5. Pour the stock mixture to the wok and stir until it thickens and forms a light glaze.
6. Put the peas and the eggs. Let the eggs poach for about 1 minute before stirring gently.
7. Sprinkle with the scallions. Serve warm.

Pan-Fried White Fish with Soy Sauce

Prep Time: 5 minutes, Cook Time: 5 minutes, Serves: 4

INGREDIENTS:
PAN-FRIED FISH:
1½ pounds (680 g) white fish fillet (cod, tilapia, or red snapper), cut into two or three pieces
1½ tbsps. peanut oil
2 tbsps. chopped scallions (optional)
1 to 2 tbsps. cornstarch
Pinch salt
Ground black pepper
SAUCE:
½ tsp. sesame oil
1 tbsp. soy sauce
½ tsp. sugar

DIRECTIONS:
1. Blot the fish dry with a paper towel. Season with salt and pepper on both sides, and dust with the cornstarch.
2. In a wok, heat the peanut oil over medium-high heat.
3. When the wok is smoking very slightly, put the fillets in the wok and leave untouched for 3 minutes.
4. Prepare the sauce by whisking together the soy sauce, sesame oil and sugar in a small bowl. Set it aside.
5. Slowly flip the fish to cook on the other side for 1 minute.
6. USe a fork to test the fish. If it flakes easily, it is cooked.
7. Remove from the heat and pour the sauce into the wok around the fish. Flip the fish one more time to coat evenly and take it to a serving plate.
8. Scatter with the chopped scallions (if using), and serve warm.

Thai White Fish and Vegetables

Prep Time: 15 minutes, Cook Time: 8 minutes, Serves: 4

INGREDIENTS:
1 pound (454 g) fresh, firm white fish fillet, cut into 1-inch pieces
3 Thai bird's eye chiles, cut into ¼-inch pieces
2 cups chopped bok choy
1 cup bean sprouts
1 onion, cut into 1-inch pieces
1 bruised lower stalk of lemongrass, outer leaves removed and stalk cut into 1-inch pieces
4 scallions, cut into 1-inch pieces
2 garlic cloves, crushed and chopped
Juice of 1 lime
2 tbsps. cooking oil
2 tbsps. rice vinegar
2 tbsps. brown sugar
1 tbsp. fish sauce
1 tbsp. mirin
1 tbsp. ginger, crushed and chopped
1 tbsp. cornstarch

DIRECTIONS:
1. Whisk together the fish sauce, mirin, rice vinegar, brown sugar, lime juice, and cornstarch in a large bowl.
2. Add the fish to the bowl and set aside to marinate when preparing the wok.
3. In a wok, heat the cooking oil over high heat until it shimmers.
4. Place the ginger, garlic, lemongrass, and onion and stir-fry for about 1 minute.
5. Remove the lemongrass and discard.
6. Put the bird's eye chiles and stir-fry for about 30 seconds.
7. Take the marinated fish to the wok, reserving the marinade, and slowly stir-fry for about 1 minute.
8. Toss in the bok choy and remaining marinade and slowly stir-fry for about 30 seconds.
9. Squeeze the scallions to bruise them, then scatter over the fish.
10. Garnish with the bean sprouts and serve hot.

Sweet Vietnamese Scallops and Cucumbers

Prep Time: 15 minutes, Cook Time: 6 minutes, Serves: 4

INGREDIENTS:

1 pound (454 g) large sea scallops, cut in half widthwise
1 European cucumber, raked and cut into ¼-inch disks
¼ cup brown sugar
¼ cup rice wine
¼ cup rice vinegar
¼ cup fish sauce
4 scallions, cut into 1-inch pieces
2 garlic cloves, crushed and chopped
Juice of 1 lime
2 tbsps. cooking oil
1 tsp. hot sesame oil

DIRECTIONS:
1. Combine the rice wine, fish sauce, brown sugar, and lime juice in a large bowl. Add the scallops to marinate and set aside.
2. In a wok, heat the cooking oil over high heat until it shimmers.
3. Add the scallions and garlic and stir-fry for about 30 seconds.
4. Place the marinated scallops, reserving the marinade, and stir-fry for about 30 seconds.
5. Then pour the cucumber and marinade to the wok and stir-fry for about 30 seconds.
6. Remove from the heat and toss the cucumbers and scallops with the sesame oil and rice vinegar. Serve warm.

Asian Stir-Fried Chili Clams

Prep Time: 5 minutes, Cook Time: 15 minutes, Serves: 4

INGREDIENTS:
SAUCE:
¼ cup water
1 tbsp. oyster sauce
2 tsps. soy sauce
½ tsp. Shaoxing wine
½ tsp. brown sugar
¼ tsp. chicken stock granules
STIR-FRY:
1½ pounds (680 g) fresh clams
1 fresh red chile, thinly sliced
2 garlic cloves, minced
2 stalks lemongrass, white portion only, halved
1 scallion, cut into 1-inch pieces
½-inch piece ginger, peeled and thinly sliced
2 tbsps. peanut oil
2 tbsps. water
1 tsp. cornstarch

DIRECTIONS:
1. Make the sauce by mixing together the water, oyster sauce, soy sauce, Shaoxing wine, brown sugar, and chicken stock granules in a small bowl. Set it aside.
2. Mix together the cornstarch and water in a separate small bowl. Set it aside.
3. In a wok, heat the peanut oil over medium-high heat.
4. Add the lemongrass and stir-fry for about 1 to 2 minutes, or until the edges start to brown a little.
5. Place the garlic and ginger and stir-fry for 20 seconds until it's fragrant.
6. Add the clams and stir in all the ingredients.
7. Stir in the sauce and let it simmer.
8. Once the clams start to open up, add the cornstarch mixture. Cover the lid if desired. By the time the sauce thickens, 20 to 30 seconds, most of the clams should be open. Discard any unopened clams.
9. Remove from the heat, and take the clams to a serving plate. Sprinkle with the red chile and scallion and serve warm.

Spicy Shrimp with Pineapple and Papaya

Prep Time: 30 minutes, Cook Time: 10 minutes, Serves: 4

INGREDIENTS:

3 cups medium large frozen shrimp, peeled, deveined, and thawed
4 to 6 cups cooked white jasmine rice
2 cups fresh pineapple, peeled, and cut into large chunks
1 whole fresh papaya, peeled, halved and seeded, cut into large chunks
1 whole fresh mango, peeled, pit removed, and cut into chunks
1⅓ cups orange juice, freshly squeezed
¼ cup granulated sugar
¼ cup white wine vinegar
4 tbsps. fresh flat leaf parsley, chopped, as garnish
4 tsps. cornstarch
2 to 3 tsps. lime juice
2 tsps. canola oil, approximately

DIRECTIONS:
1. Add the vinegar and cornstarch and beat in a bowl till smooth.
2. In a large wok over medium-high heat, heat the oil and stir fry the shrimp for 5 minutes.
3. Transfer the shrimp into a bowl with a slotted spoon and set aside.
4. In the same wok, stir together the lime juice, orange juice, sugar, pineapple, papaya and mango.
5. Pour in the cornstarch mixture, stirring constantly and bring to a boil.
6. Cook, stirring constantly for 1 minute.
7. Put the shrimp and cook for 1 minute, stirring continuously.
8. Quickly remove from the heat.
9. Pour the shrimp mixture over the hot cooked rice and garnish with the parsley.

Light Seafood Congee

Prep Time: 10 minutes, Cook Time: 1 hour, Serves: 4 to 6

INGREDIENTS:
- 1 (¾-pound / 340-g) cod, tilapia, or halibut fillet, cut into bite-size pieces
- 6 to 8 large shrimp, each cut into two or three pieces
- 1 cup short-grain rice, rinsed and drained
- ½ cup bay scallops
- 6 cups water, plus more for rinsing rice
- ½ cup fresh cilantro leaves
- 2-inch piece ginger, peeled, plus 1-inch piece, julienned, for garnish
- 1 scallion, chopped
- 2 tsps. sesame oil
- 2 tsps. salt

DIRECTIONS:
1. In a large pot, add the rice, 6 cups of water and peeled ginger.
2. Bring the water to a boil then low the heat.
3. Simmer, partially uncovered, for 1 hour, stirring frequently to prevent sticking.
4. Increase the heat to medium and season with the salt. Place the fish, shrimp and scallops into the congee. Slowly stir to distribute the seafood evenly. Cook for about 2 minutes, remove from the heat and stir in the sesame oil.
5. Serve hot with the chopped scallion, cilantro leaves and julienned ginger on the side.

Quick Shrimp with Lobster Sauce

Prep Time: 5 minutes, Cook Time: 5 minutes, Serves: 4 to 6

INGREDIENTS:
SAUCE:
- 2 tsps. cornstarch
- 2 tsps. soy sauce
- 1 cup chicken stock
- ½ tsp. sugar
- 1 tsp. Shaoxing wine
- Pinch ground white pepper

STIR-FRY:
- 1 pound (454 g) large shrimp, peeled and deveined
- ½ cup frozen peas and carrots
- 1 egg, lightly beaten
- 1 tbsp. peanut oil
- 2 garlic cloves, minced
- 2-inch piece ginger, peeled and julienned

DIRECTIONS:
1. Prepare the sauce by combining the chicken stock, soy sauce, cornstarch, Shaoxing wine, sugar, and pepper in a small bowl. Stir well and break up any lumps. Set it aside.
2. In a wok, heat the peanut oil over medium-high heat.
3. Place the ginger and garlic and stir-fry until aromatic, or for 20 seconds.
4. Put the frozen peas and carrots and stir-fry for about 10 seconds.
5. Add the sauce and the shrimp. Stir to combine all the ingredients with a wok spatula.
6. Gently pour in the beaten egg while swirl it into the sauce with the wok spatula.
7. Once the shrimp are cooked (they curl into a "C" shape), take the dish to a serving plate and serve hot.

Bay Scallops with Snow Peas

Prep Time: 10 minutes, Cook Time: 10 minutes, Serves: 4 to 6

INGREDIENTS:
SAUCE:
- 2 tbsps. water
- 1 tbsp. oyster sauce
- 1 tsp. soy sauce
- ½ tsp. sesame oil
- ½ tsp. sugar

STIR-FRY:
- 1 pound (454 g) fresh bay scallops
- ¾ pound (340 g) snow peas, trimmed and strings removed
- 2-inch piece ginger, peeled and minced
- 2 garlic cloves, minced
- 2½ tbsps. peanut oil, divided
- 1 tbsp. water
- 1 tsp. cornstarch
- ½ tsp. salt
- Pinch sugar
- Pinch ground white pepper

DIRECTIONS:
1. Prepare the sauce by combining the water, oyster sauce, soy sauce, sugar and sesame oil in a small bowl. Set it aside.
2. Mix together the water and cornstarch in a separate small bowl. Set it aside.
3. Rinse the scallops and blot them dry with paper towel. Season them with salt, pepper and pinch of sugar.
4. In a wok, heat 1½ tbsps. of peanut oil over medium-high heat.
5. Place the scallops and stir-fry for 4 minutes. Remove the scallops and set them aside.
6. Pour the remaining 1 tbsp. of peanut oil to the wok. Put the ginger and garlic and stir-fry until aromatic, or for 30 seconds.
7. Arrange the snow peas and stir-fry until bright green, for 1 minute. Stir in the sauce.
8. When the snow peas have softened, pour in the cornstarch mixture. Stir-fry until the sauce begins to thicken.
9. Take the scallops back to the wok and after a very quick stir-fry, transfer the scallops to a serving plate. Serve warm.

Chapter 7 Fish and Seafood

Simple Ginger and Scallion Crab

Prep Time: 10 minutes, Cook Time: 5 minutes, Serves: 4 to 6

INGREDIENTS:
SAUCE:
1½ tbsps. oyster sauce
4 tbsps. water
1 tsp. soy sauce
½ tsp. sesame oil
½ tsp. cornstarch
½ tsp. sugar
Pinch ground white pepper
STIR-FRY:
4 whole Dungeness or blue crabs (about 2 pounds / 907 g each), cooked, cleaned, and cut
2-inch piece ginger, peeled and sliced
2 scallions, cut into 1-inch pieces
1 tbsp. peanut oil

DIRECTIONS:
1. Make the sauce by mixing together the water, oyster sauce, soy sauce, sesame oil, sugar, cornstarch and pepper in a small bowl.
2. Add the peanut oil into the wok along with the ginger slices. Turn the heat to medium-high. Stir-fry the ginger slices until it is fragrant.
3. Pour the crab and the sauce to the wok. Toss to coat the crab with the sauce evenly.
4. Once the sauce thickens, remove from the heat and add the scallions. Stir-fry for a few seconds.
5. Take the crab to a serving dish and serve warm.

Teriyaki Salmon with Sugar Snap

Prep Time: 15 minutes, Cook Time: 8 minutes, Serves: 4

INGREDIENTS:
1 pound (454 g) thick, center-cut salmon fillet, cut into 1-inch pieces
2 cups sugar snap or snow pea pods
4 ounces (113 g) shiitake mushrooms, cut into slices
1 medium onion, diced
2 garlic cloves, crushed and chopped
2 scallions, cut into 1-inch pieces
2 tbsps. cooking oil
2 tbsps. honey
2 tbsps. tamari
2 tbsps. mirin
2 tbsps. rice vinegar
1 tbsp. ginger, crushed and chopped
1 tbsp. sesame seeds
1 tbsp. white miso

DIRECTIONS:
1. Whisk together the tamari, honey, mirin, rice vinegar and miso in a large bowl. Place the salmon, making sure to coat evenly with the marinade, and set aside.
2. In a wok, heat the cooking oil over high heat until it shimmers.
3. Add the ginger, garlic and onion and stir-fry for about 1 minute.
4. Place the mushrooms and pea pods and stir-fry for 1 minute.
5. Then add the marinated salmon, reserving the marinade, and slowly stir-fry for about 1 minute.
6. Toss in the marinade and scallions and slowly stir-fry for 30 seconds.
7. Scatter the sesame seeds on top. Serve hot.

Chinese Steamed Fish

Prep Time: 10 minutes, Cook Time: 7 minutes, Serves: 4

INGREDIENTS:
SAUCE:
1 tsp. sesame oil
2 tbsps. soy sauce
½ tsp. sugar
2 tsps. Shaoxing wine
1 tbsp. water
Pinch ground white pepper
STEAMED FISH:
1½ pounds (680 g) white fish fillet (such as cod or red snapper)
¼ cup fresh cilantro leaves
2-inch piece ginger, peeled, half sliced and half julienned
2 scallions, julienned
1 tbsp. peanut oil
1 tsp. sesame oil
½ tsp. salt
2 pinches ground white pepper

DIRECTIONS:
1. Make the sauce by combining the soy sauce, water, Shaoxing wine, sesame oil, sugar, and pepper in a small bowl. Set it aside.
2. In a wok, set up a metal steaming rack and pour water into the wok halfway up to the bottom of the steaming plate. Turn the heat to medium-high.
3. Brush the sesame oil over the entire surface of the fish fillet and season the both sides with salt and pepper.
4. Put the fish fillet on a heatproof dish and place the sliced ginger on top of the fish.
5. Cover and steam for about 5 minutes or until the fish is cooked completely (it should flake easily with a fork).
6. Take the fish to a serving plate, discarding the ginger slices.
7. Discard the water from the wok, then return the wok to the burner and dry over medium heat.
8. When the wok has completely dried, pour the peanut oil to the wok followed by the julienned ginger. Once the ginger starts to turn golden brown, add the sauce. Let the sauce boil for just a few seconds, then spoon the sauce over the fish with a wok spatula or ladle.
9. Sprinkle with the scallions and cilantro leaves, and serve warm.

Korean Spicy Stir-Fry Squid

Prep Time: 15 minutes, Cook Time: 5 minutes, Serves: 4

INGREDIENTS:
½ pound (227 g) small to medium squid tentacles and rings, rinsed in cold water
4 ounces (113 g) shiitake mushrooms, cut into slices
2 baby bok choy, leaves separated
1 medium red onion, cut into 1-inch pieces
2 Thai bird's eye chiles, cut into ¼-inch circles
4 scallions, cut into 1-inch pieces
2 garlic cloves, crushed and chopped
2 tbsps. soy sauce
2 tbsps. rice wine
2 tbsps. gochujang
2 tbsps. brown sugar
2 tbsps. cooking oil
1 tbsp. ginger, crushed and chopped
1 tbsp. sesame seeds
1 tsp. hot sesame oil

DIRECTIONS:
1. In a wok, heat the cooking oil over high heat until it shimmers.
2. Add the ginger, garlic and onion and stir-fry for about 1 minute.
3. Place the mushrooms and bok choy and stir-fry for 1 minute.
4. Then put the squid and bird's eye chiles and stir-fry for about 30 seconds.
5. Toss the rice wine, soy sauce, gochujang and brown sugar and stir-fry for about 30 seconds.
6. Pour in the sesame oil, sesame seeds and scallions and stir-fry for about 30 seconds.
7. Serve hot.

Japanese Miso Cod with Tea Rice

Prep Time: 15 minutes, Cook Time: 25 minutes, Serves: 4

INGREDIENTS:
1 pound (454 g) "captain's cut" (very thick) cod, cut into 4 pieces
2 cups genmaicha green tea
1 cup uncooked rice
3 garlic cloves, crushed and chopped
2 scallions cut into ½-inch pieces, for garnish
2 tbsps. white miso
2 tbsps. cooking oil
2 tbsps. honey
2 tbsps. tamari
2 tbsps. mirin
1 tbsp. toasted sesame oil
1 tbsp. sesame seeds

DIRECTIONS:
1. Prepare the rice as package directions, using genmaicha green tea instead of water.
2. Whisk together the miso, tamari, mirin, honey and sesame oil in a large bowl. Place the cod and coat evenly with the marinade, then set aside.
3. In a wok, heat the cooking oil over high heat until it shimmers.
4. Add the garlic and stir-fry for about 30 seconds until browned.
5. Place the marinated cod in the wok, reserving the marinade, and fry for about 30 seconds per side, flipping slowly.
6. Toss in the marinade and fry the fish for another 30 seconds on each side.
7. Sprinkle with the sesame seeds and scallions and serve warm.

Stir-Fry Shrimp and Broccoli

Prep Time: 15 minutes, Cook Time: 5 minutes, Serves: 6 to 8

INGREDIENTS:
MARINADE:
½ pound (227 g) large shrimp, peeled and deveined
2 tsps. cornstarch
1 tsp. Shaoxing wine
½ tsp. salt
Pinch ground white pepper
SAUCE:
2 tsps. rice vinegar
2 tsps. oyster sauce
2 tbsps. soy sauce
½ tsp. sugar
½ tsp. sesame oil
STIR-FRY:
2 heads broccoli, cut into florets
1 carrot, peeled and sliced
1-inch piece ginger, peeled and julienned
2 garlic cloves, minced
1 scallion, chopped
1 tbsp. peanut oil
1 tsp. toasted sesame seeds

DIRECTIONS:
1. In a medium bowl, add the Shaoxing wine, cornstarch, salt and pepper over the shrimp and toss to combine well. Marinate the shrimp at room temperature for about 10 minutes.
2. At the same time, make the sauce by combining the oyster sauce, soy sauce, rice vinegar, sesame oil and sugar in a small bowl.
3. In a wok, heat the peanut oil over medium-high heat.
4. Place the ginger and garlic, and stir-fry until aromatic, or for 20 seconds. Arrange the carrot and broccoli florets, and stir-fry for 1 minute.
5. Put the shrimp and the sauce to the wok. Stir-fry until the shrimp are cooked completely and the vegetables have softened.
6. Scatter the sesame seeds over the dish and stir to combine well.
7. Remove from the heat, garnish with the scallion and serve hot.

French Inspired Halibut

Prep Time: 10 minutes, Cook Time: 15 minutes, Serves: 4

INGREDIENTS:

2 (8-ounce / 227-g) halibut steaks
½ cup white wine
¼ cup butter
3 tbsps. capers, with liquid vinegar
1 tbsp. olive oil
1 tsp. chopped garlic
Salt and pepper to taste

DIRECTIONS:

1. In a large wok over medium-high heat, heat the olive oil and fry the halibut steaks until browned from all sides.
2. Transfer the halibut steaks into a bowl and set aside.
3. In the same pan, add the wine and scrape any browned bits from the bottom with a spatula.
4. Cook until the wine is almost absorbed.
5. Toss in the garlic, capers, butter, salt and pepper and simmer for about 1 minute.
6. Stir in the steaks and cook until the fish flakes easily with a fork.
7. Pour the sauce over the fish. Serve warm.

Sichuan Mussels and Shrimp

Prep Time: 15 minutes, Cook Time: 6 minutes, Serves: 4

INGREDIENTS:

1 pound (454 g) mussels, cleaned and rinsed
½ pound (227 g) large shrimp, with or without shells
¼ cup oyster sauce
¼ cup rice wine
¼ cup vegetable or meat broth
4 garlic cloves, crushed and chopped
2 tbsps. cooking oil
2 tbsps. Chinese five-spice powder
2 tbsps. ginger, crushed and chopped
1 tbsp. red pepper flakes

DIRECTIONS:

1. In a wok, heat the cooking oil over high heat until it shimmers.
2. Add the ginger and garlic and stir-fry until lightly browned.
3. Place the shrimp and stir-fry for about 1 minute.
4. Pour the rice wine, five-spice powder, red pepper and broth and bring to a boil.
5. Then put the mussels, cover the lid and cook for about 2 minutes, or until the mussels open.
6. Uncover the lid and stir the ingredients for about 1 minute, mixing well.
7. Pour the oyster sauce over the mussels and shrimp. Serve warm.

Malaysian Chili Squid and Celery

Prep Time: 15 minutes, Cook Time: 5 minutes, Serves: 4

INGREDIENTS:

½ pound (227 g) small to medium squid tentacles and rings, rinsed in cold water
3 stalks celery, cut diagonally into ¼-inch pieces
2 chiles, cut into ¼-inch pieces
2 garlic cloves, crushed and chopped
½ cup oyster sauce
2 tbsps. cooking oil
2 tbsps. rice wine
1 tsp. hot sesame oil

DIRECTIONS:

1. In a wok, heat the cooking oil over high heat until it shimmers.
2. Add the celery and garlic and stir-fry for about 1 minute.
3. Pour in the squid and rice wine and stir-fry for about 1 minute.
4. Then place the chiles and stir-fry for about 30 seconds.
5. Toss the sesame oil and oyster sauce and stir-fry for about 30 seconds.
6. Serve hot.

Easy Salt and Pepper Shrimp

Prep Time: 5 minutes, Cook Time: 5 minutes, Serves: 4 to 6

INGREDIENTS:

1 pound (454 g) large shrimp, deveined, tail on
½ jalapeño or 1 Thai bird's eye chile, thinly sliced (optional)
1 sprig fresh cilantro, roughly chopped
3 tbsps. cornstarch
2 tbsps. peanut oil
1 tsp. sea salt
1 tsp. freshly ground black pepper

DIRECTIONS:

1. Combine the cornstarch, pepper and sea salt in a medium bowl. Mix well and set it aside.
2. Place the shrimp to the cornstarch mixture and toss to coat well before frying the shrimp.
3. In a wok, heat the peanut oil over medium-high heat.
4. Carefully shake any excess cornstarch off the shrimp and put them in the wok in a single layer.
5. Let the shrimp cook on one side for 30 seconds before flipping.
6. Arrange the sliced jalapeño or chile (if using) to the wok and slowly stir-fry to combine.
7. Take the shrimp to a serving dish and garnish with the cilantro.

Mussels with Tomato Sauce

Prep Time: 20 minutes, Cook Time: 25 minutes, Serves: 4

INGREDIENTS:

1 pound (454 g) mussels, cleaned and debearded
3 cups canned tomato sauce
1 cup chopped green onions
2 tbsps. minced garlic
2 tbsps. minced shallots
1 tbsp. butter
1 tbsp. olive oil
1 tbsp. capers
1 tbsp. Italian seasoning
½ tsp. red pepper flakes

DIRECTIONS:

1. In a wok over medium heat, heat the oil and butter. Sauté the shallots, garlic and capers for 5 minutes.
2. Toss in the tomato sauce, Italian herbs and red pepper flakes and reduce the heat to medium-low.
3. Cover and simmer for 10 minutes.
4. Stir in the mussels and increase the heat to medium-high.
5. Cook, covered for 10 minutes.
6. Scoop out and discard any unopened mussels from the wok.
7. Garnish the green onions and serve warm.

Salmon and Vegetables with Oyster Sauce

Prep Time: 15 minutes, Cook Time: 6 minutes, Serves: 4

INGREDIENTS:

1 pound (454 g) thick, center-cut salmon fillet, cut into 1-inch pieces
2 baby bok choy, leaves separated
1 red onion, cut into 1-inch pieces
1 red bell pepper, cut into 1-inch pieces
½ cup oyster sauce
4 scallions, cut into ½-inch pieces
2 garlic cloves, crushed and chopped
2 tbsps. cooking oil
2 tbsps. rice wine
1 tbsp. crushed and chopped ginger

DIRECTIONS:

1. Whisk together the oyster sauce and rice wine in a large bowl. Add the salmon and allow to marinate while you stir-fry.
2. In a wok, heat the cooking oil over high heat until it shimmers.
3. Add the ginger, garlic and onion and stir-fry for about 1 minute.
4. Place the salmon, reserving the marinade, and slowly stir-fry for about 1 minute.
5. Then put the bell pepper and bok choy and stir-fry for about 1 minute.
6. Pour the reserved marinade and scallions to the wok and slowly stir-fry for about 1 minute. Serve warm.

Garlic King Crab with Hoisin Sauce

Prep Time: 15 minutes, Cook Time: 6 minutes, Serves: 4

INGREDIENTS:

2 pounds (907 g) king crab legs, cut into 2-inch sections and left in the shell
1 cup fish or lobster broth
¼ cup hoisin sauce
3 garlic cloves, crushed and chopped
4 scallions, cut into ½-inch pieces
3 tbsps. cooking oil
2 tbsps. rice wine
2 tbsps. cornstarch
2 tbsps. ginger, crushed and chopped

DIRECTIONS:

1. Whisk together the broth, rice wine and cornstarch in a small bowl. Set aside.
2. In a wok, heat the cooking oil over high heat until it shimmers.
3. Add the garlic and ginger and stir-fry for about 1 minute.
4. Place the crab legs and stir-fry for about 1 minute.
5. Pour in the broth mixture and stir-fry for about 1 minute.
6. Toss the hoisin sauce and stir-fry until a glaze forms.
7. Squeeze the scallions to bruise them, then scatter them into the wok to garnish the crab.
8. Serve hot.

Seafood Salad, page 43

South American Pasta and Beef Salad, page 45

Steak with Arugula Salad, page 45

Savory Bean and Tomato Salad, page 43

Chapter 8 Salads

Seafood Salad

Prep Time: 20 minutes, Cook Time: 5 minutes, Serves: 2

INGREDIENTS:
1½ cups cooked lobster meat, chopped
2 cups iceberg lettuce, torn
¼ cup feta cheese, crumbled
1 tomato, chopped
½ of avocado, peeled, pitted and chopped
2 tbsps. butter
1 tsp. seafood seasoning

DIRECTIONS:
1. In a wok over medium heat, melt the butter.
2. Place the lobster meat and cook for 2 to 3 minutes or till just heated.
3. Toss in the seafood seasoning and quickly remove from heat.
4. Transfer the lobster meat to a large serving bowl.
5. Put the remaining ingredients except the feta cheese and slowly toss to coat well.
6. Top with the cheese and enjoy!

Savory Bean and Tomato Salad

Prep Time: 15 minutes, Cook Time: 10 minutes, Serves: 4

INGREDIENTS:
1 (15-ounce / 425-g) can cannellini beans, drained and rinsed
1 (14½-ounce / 411-g) can diced tomatoes
3 cups arugula
¼ cup shaved Parmesan cheese (optional)
2 cloves garlic, minced
3 tbsps. white wine
2 tbsps. olive oil
2 tbsps. chopped fresh basil
1 tsp. dried sage
1 tsp. dried thyme
Salt and pepper to taste

DIRECTIONS:
1. In a large wok over medium heat, heat the oil and sauté the garlic for 1 minute.
2. Place the wine, tomatoes, thyme and sage and stir to combine well.
3. Increase the heat to medium-high and cook for about 2 to 3 minutes.
4. Toss the basil, cannellini beans, salt and black pepper and cook for about 3 to 4 minutes.
5. Spread the arugula onto a serving platter and place the beans on top.
6. Garnish with the Parmesan cheese and serve hot.

Simple Myriam's Salad

Prep Time: 10 minutes, Cook Time: 25 minutes, Serves: 2

INGREDIENTS:
2 vine ripened tomatoes
3 large green bell peppers
1 to 2 garlic cloves, minced
1 tsp. olive oil
Salt

DIRECTIONS:
1. Arrange the bell peppers on the stove and grill them until they turn black.
2. Take them to a plastic bag and seal it. Allow it to rest for about 5 to 6 minutes.
3. Once the time is up, peel, rinse and chop the peppers.
4. In a wok, heat the oil over medium heat.
5. Toss the tomatoes with peppers and garlic. Cook them for about 3 minutes.
6. Season with a pinch of salt and cook them for about 16 minutes while frequently stirring.
7. Serve your salad warm.

Peppery Bean and Spinach Salad

Prep Time: 10 minutes, Cook Time: 25 minutes, Serves: 4

INGREDIENTS:
1 (15-ounce / 425-g) can black beans, drained
1 (10-ounce / 283-g) bag fresh baby spinach
1 (10-ounce / 283-g) can diced tomatoes with green chile
1 onion, thinly sliced
2 cloves garlic, chopped
2 tbsps. extra-virgin olive oil
½ tsp. red pepper flakes
1 tsp. kosher salt
½ tsp. ground black pepper

DIRECTIONS:
1. In a large wok over medium-high heat, heat the oil and cook the onion with salt for 10 to 15 minutes.
2. Toss the red pepper, garlic and black pepper and cook for 1 minute.
3. Stir in the black beans and tomatoes and cook for 5 minutes.
4. Turn off the heat and gently stir in the spinach.
5. Set aside, covered for about 3 minutes.
6. Toss the mixture well and serve quickly.

Turkey and Bean Salad

Prep Time: 15 minutes, Cook Time: 15 minutes, Serves: 4

INGREDIENTS:

1 tbsp. vegetable oil
1 pound (454 g) ground turkey
1 (14-ounce / 397-g) can black beans, drained
1 (15-ounce / 425-g) can corn, drained
4 green onions, chopped (optional)
⅓ cup shredded Cheddar cheese
¼ cup spicy ranch-style salad dressing
1 head lettuce, chopped
1 avocado, peeled, pitted, and diced
1 small white onion, diced
1 (1-ounce / 28-g) package taco seasoning mix

DIRECTIONS:

1. In a wok over medium heat, heat oil and sauté the white onion for 5 minutes.
2. Break ground turkey into small chunks with your hands.
3. Place the turkey into the wok and cook for 2 to 3 minutes.
4. Add the taco seasoning and cook for 5 to 7 minutes.
5. Turn off the heat and set aside to cool slightly.
6. In a large salad bowl, arrange the lettuce and top with the turkey mixture, followed by the black beans, corn, avocado, green onions, Cheddar cheese and spicy ranch dressing.

Tuna and Beans Salad

Prep Time: 10 minutes, Cook Time: 5 minutes, Serves: 4

INGREDIENTS:

¾ pound (340 g) green beans, trimmed and snapped in half
1 (16-ounce / 454-g) can Great Northern beans, drained and rinsed
1 (12-ounce / 340-g) can solid white albacore tuna, drained
1 (2¼-ounce / 64-g) can sliced black olives, drained
¼ medium red onion, thinly sliced
6 tbsps. extra-virgin olive oil
3 tbsps. lemon juice
1 tsp. dried oregano
½ tsp. finely grated lemon zest
Salt, to taste

DIRECTIONS:

1. In a medium wok over high heat, place the green beans, ⅓ cup water and a large pinch of salt and bring to a boil.
2. Cook the beans for 5 minutes.
3. Immediately, take the mixture onto a paper towels lined cookie sheet and set aside to cool.
4. Mix together the Great Northern beans, tuna, olives and onion in a bowl.
5. Add the oil, lemon juice, oregano and lemon zest in another bowl and beat till well combined.
6. Pour dressing over the salad and slowly stir to combine.
7. Serve hot.

Butternut Squash and Bean Salad

Prep Time: 15 minutes, Cook Time: 35 minutes, Serves: 8

INGREDIENTS:

2 (15-ounce / 425-g) cans cannellini beans, drained and rinsed
1 cup peeled, seeded, and diced butternut squash
1 cup chopped baby broccoli
3 slices bacon, cooked and crumbled
1 red onion, chopped
¼ cup chicken stock
3 tbsps. maple syrup, divided
3 tbsps. olive oil, divided
½ tsp. dried thyme leaves

DIRECTIONS:

1. In a wok over low heat, place the cannellini beans and cook till heated through.
2. In a wok over medium heat, heat 1 tbsp. of the olive oil and cook the red onion for 5 minutes.
3. Add 1 tbsp. of the maple syrup and stir to combine well.
4. Reduce the heat to medium-low and simmer for 15 minutes, stirring frequently.
5. Turn off the heat and transfer the onion mixture into beans.
6. In the same wok over medium heat, heat 1 more tbsp. olive oil and cook the butternut squash for 8 minutes. Add 1 tbsp. of the maple syrup and cook for 5 minutes.
7. Remove from the heat and transfer the squash mixture into beans.
8. In the same wok, heat the remaining 1 tbsp. of the olive oil on medium heat and cook the broccoli for 7 minutes.
9. Remove from the heat and transfer the broccoli into beans.
10. Place the chicken stock into the bean mixture and increase the heat to medium-low.
11. Toss in the remaining 1 tbsp. of the maple syrup and thyme and bring to a gentle boil.
12. Simmer till heated completely, stirring slowly. Top with the crumbled bacon.

Chapter 8 Salads

South American Pasta and Beef Salad

Prep Time: 10 minutes, Cook Time: 20 minutes, Serves: 6

INGREDIENTS:
1 pound (454 g) ground beef
3 cups shredded lettuce
2 cups spiral pasta
2 cups halved cherry tomatoes
1 cup shredded Cheddar cheese
1 (7-ounce / 198-g) bag corn chips
½ cup chopped onion
½ cup French salad dressing
1 (1¼-ounce / 35-g) package taco seasoning
2 tbsps. sour cream

DIRECTIONS:
1. Cook the pasta in salty boiling water for 10 minutes until soft before draining it.
2. In a large wok, cook the ground beef for 10 minutes or until it is no longer pink from the center before stirring in taco seasoning.
3. Coat the mixture of pasta and beef with the lettuce, French dressing, tomatoes, Cheddar cheese, onion and corn chips very thoroughly, then refrigerate for at least 2 hours.
4. Pour some sour cream at the top and serve.

Steak with Arugula Salad

Prep Time: 10 minutes, Cook Time: 15 minutes, Serves: 4

INGREDIENTS:
4 boneless strip steaks, 1 to 1¼ inches thick
8 cups loosely packed arugula, washed and dried
3 ounces (85 g) Parmesan cheese, cut into thin shavings
2 garlic cloves, minced
5 tbsps. extra virgin olive oil, plus 1 tsp.
1 tbsp. fresh-squeezed lemon juice
1 tbsp. chopped fresh parsley
1 tbsp. chopped fresh oregano
Pinch of salt
Fresh coarse ground black pepper

DIRECTIONS:
1. In a small bowl, whisk the 5 tbsps. of olive oil with lemon juice, parsley, garlic, oregano and a pinch each of salt and pepper.
2. In a large wok over medium-high heat, heat 1 tsp. of oil.
3. Sprinkle the steaks strips with some salt and pepper. Cook them for about 7 minutes on each side.
4. Spread the arugula leaves in 4 serving plates then put the steaks strips, lemon dressing and cheese on top. Serve your salads immediately.

Roasted Red Pepper and Edamame Salad

Prep Time: 20 minutes, Cook Time: 10 minutes, Serves: 12

INGREDIENTS:
1 (16-ounce / 454-g) package frozen shelled edamame (green soybeans)
1 (16-ounce / 454-g) package frozen corn
1 (15-ounce / 425-g) can black beans, rinsed and drained
1 (15-ounce / 425-g) can garbanzo beans, drained
1 (12-ounce / 340-g) jar roasted red peppers, drained and chopped
1 sweet onion, diced
¼ cup chopped fresh cilantro
2 tbsps. freshly squeezed lime juice
1 tsp. ground cumin
1 tsp. smoked sea salt

DIRECTIONS:
1. In a large nonstick wok on medium-high heat, cook the frozen corn for 5 minutes, stirring frequently.
2. Place the onion and cook for 5 minutes.
3. Stir in the garbanzo beans, black beans, edamame, roasted red pepper, cumin and salt and cook for 3 to 5 minutes.
4. Turn off the heat and toss in the cilantro and lime juice.
5. Serve hot.

Simple Sweet Peanut Soup, page 47

Chinese Chicken Stock, page 48

Chicken and Vegetables Stir-Fry Soup, page 51

Ginger Egg Drop Soup, page 48

46   Chapter 9 Soups and Stews

Chapter 9 Soups and Stews

Simple Sweet Peanut Soup

Prep Time: 5 minutes, Cook Time: 2 hours, Serves: 4 to 6

INGREDIENTS:
½ pound (227 g) raw peanuts, shelled and skinned
8 cups water, plus more for soaking
4 tbsps. sugar
1 tbsp. baking soda

DIRECTIONS:
1. In a bowl of water, soak the peanuts overnight.
2. Rinse the peanuts, pour in the baking soda, then cover in fresh water to soak for 1 to 2 more hours.
3. Rinse the peanuts thoroughly.
4. In a wok, bring the 8 cups of water to a boil over high heat.
5. Place the peanuts to the boiling water, reduce the heat to low, and simmer, partially covered, for about 2 hours.
6. Put the sugar in increments until the soup reaches your desired sweetness.
7. Serve the soup warm.

Stir-Fried Bok Choy, Egg and Tofu Soup

Prep Time: 15 minutes, Cook Time: 8 minutes, Serves: 4

INGREDIENTS:
1 pound (454 g) tofu, well drained, patted dry, and cut into 1-inch pieces
1 cup chopped bok choy
4 eggs, beaten
4 ounces (113 g) mushrooms, cut into slices
1 red bell pepper, cut into ¼-inch pieces
2 quarts vegetable or meat broth
2 garlic cloves, crushed and chopped
2 tbsps. cooking oil
1 tbsp. ginger, crushed and chopped
1 tsp. hot sesame oil

DIRECTIONS:
1. In a wok, heat the cooking oil over high heat until it shimmers.
2. Add the ginger, garlic, and tofu and stir-fry until the tofu begins to brown.
3. Place the bell pepper and stir-fry for about 1 minute.
4. Then put the mushrooms and bok choy and stir-fry for about 30 seconds.
5. Add the sesame oil and broth and bring to a boil.
6. Drizzle the beaten eggs over the broth and allow the eggs to float to the top. Serve hot.

Pork and Shrimp Wonton Soup

Prep Time: 20 minutes, Cook Time: 10 minutes, Serves: 6 to 8

INGREDIENTS:
WONTONS:
20 to 25 square wonton wrappers
¼ pound (113 g) ground pork
¼ pound (113 g) shrimp, peeled, deveined, and roughly chopped
1 tsp. sesame oil
1 tsp. cornstarch
1 tsp. soy sauce
½ tsp. salt
Pinch ground white pepper
SOUP:
8 cups chicken stock
1 scallion, chopped
2 tbsps. low-sodium soy sauce
2 tsps. sesame oil
3 pinches ground white pepper

DIRECTIONS:
MAKE THE WONTONS:
1. Mix together the pork, shrimp, cornstarch, sesame oil, soy sauce, salt and pepper in a bowl.
2. Put about 1 tsp. of pork mixture in the center of a wonton wrapper.
3. Use water to dampen your finger and run it along the edge of the wonton to help seal it, then fold the wonton in half into a triangle. Slowly press the edges to seal.
4. Fold the bottom two corners (just outside the meat filling) toward each other, and press those corners together to seal them. Keep the wontons aside.
MAKE THE SOUP:
5. In a wok over high heat, bring the chicken stock to a boil. Place the soy sauce and sesame oil.
6. Bring a separate pot of water to a boil. Slowly drop the wontons into the boiling water.
7. Once the wontons are cooked, they will float to the top. When they all float to the top, continue boiling for about 2 minutes to cook them all the way through.
8. Carefully transfer the wontons from the water to the chicken stock with a skimmer.
9. Place the pepper and scallion just before serving.

Chinese Chicken Stock

Prep Time: 5 minutes, Cook Time: 3 to 4 hours, Makes: 8 to 13 cups

INGREDIENTS:

10 to 15 cups water
1 whole chicken
1 large yellow onion, peeled and halved
2 large carrots, peeled and quartered
3 scallions
2-inch piece ginger, peeled

DIRECTIONS:

1. In a wok, add the chicken, carrots, onion, ginger and scallions.
2. Cover the chicken with just enough water in the wok.
3. Simmer on low heat for about 3 to 4 hours, partially uncovered. Remove any froth from the surface and any excess oil with an ultra-fine mesh skimmer.
4. Let the stock cool slightly then remove the solid ingredients.
5. Run the stock through a fine mesh strainer as you pour it into storage jars or containers. You can scoop off the solidified fat through refrigerating the stock overnight.

Chinese Mushroom and Carrot Soup

Prep Time: 10 minutes, Cook Time: 25 minutes, Serves: 6 to 8

INGREDIENTS:

5 or 6 white or brown button mushrooms, cut into thin slices
4 or 5 large shiitake mushrooms, cut into thin slices
1 small bunch enoki mushrooms, roots removed
1 carrot, cut into thin slices
¼ cup dried goji berries
½ onion, sliced
8 cups vegetable stock
2 garlic cloves, minced
1 tbsp. olive oil
1 tbsp. soy sauce
2 tsps. sesame oil
1 tsp. salt

DIRECTIONS:

1. In a wok, heat the olive oil over medium heat.
2. Cook the onion and garlic until the onion become slightly translucent.
3. Place the carrot, button mushrooms, shiitake mushrooms, and enoki mushrooms. Cook for about 1 minute.
4. Pour in the vegetable stock and bring to a boil over medium-high heat.
5. Place the sesame oil, goji berries, soy sauce and salt.
6. Simmer over low heat for 20 minutes before serving.

Tomato and Egg Drop Soup

Prep Time: 10 minutes, Cook Time: 10 minutes, Serves: 4

INGREDIENTS:

2 eggs, lightly beaten
1 medium tomato, diced
4 cups chicken stock
1 scallion, chopped
3 tbsps. water
1½ tbsps. cornstarch
1 tsp. salt
Pinch ground white pepper

DIRECTIONS:

1. Combine the cornstarch and water in a small bowl.
2. In a wok, bring the chicken stock to a boil over medium-high heat. Season with the salt.
3. Stir in the cornstarch-water mixture. Return to a boil.
4. Swirl the soup with a pair of chopsticks, and at the same time slowly pour the beaten eggs into the soup. Swirl faster for a thinner, silky egg consistency; or slower for a thicker, chunky egg consistency.
5. Place the tomato and pepper, stir and simmer for about 1 minute.
6. Sprinkle with the scallion and serve hot.

Ginger Egg Drop Soup

Prep Time: 5 minutes, Cook Time: 10 minutes, Serves: 4

INGREDIENTS:

2 large eggs, lightly beaten
4 cups low-sodium chicken broth
2 peeled fresh ginger slices, each about the size of a quarter
2 scallions, thinly sliced, for garnish
2 garlic cloves, peeled
3 tbsps. water
2 tbsps. cornstarch
2 tsps. light soy sauce
1 tsp. sesame oil

DIRECTIONS:

1. In a wok over high heat, combine the broth, garlic, ginger, and light soy and bring to a boil. Reduce to a simmer and cook for about 5 minutes. Remove the ginger and garlic and discard.
2. Mix the cornstarch and water in a small bowl and stir the mixture into the wok. Lower the heat to medium-high and stir for 30 seconds, until the soup thickens.
3. Reduce the heat to a simmer. Dip a fork into the beaten eggs and then drag it through the soup, slowly stirring as you go. Continue to dip the fork into the egg and drag it through the soup to make the egg threads. Once all the egg has been added, simmer the soup undisturbed for a few moments to set the eggs. Drizzle in the sesame oil and scoop the soup into serving bowls. Sprinkle with the scallions and serve.

Chapter 9 Soups and Stews

Hot and Sour Noodle with Pork Soup

Prep Time: 15 minutes, Cook Time: 8 minutes, Serves: 4

INGREDIENTS:

8 ounces (227 g) dry vermicelli glass noodles
½ pound (227 g) ground pork
4 eggs, cracked into a bowl with yolks unbroken
1 cup chopped bok choy
1 medium carrot, julienned
¼ cup rice vinegar
3 quarts meat or vegetable broth
2 garlic cloves, crushed and chopped
1 scallion, cut into ½-inch pieces
2 tbsps. cooking oil
1 tbsp. ginger, crushed and chopped
1 tsp. hot sesame oil

DIRECTIONS:

1. In a wok, heat the cooking oil over high heat until it shimmers.
2. Add the garlic, ginger, pork, and carrot and stir-fry for about 1 minute.
3. Pour the broth, noodles, sesame oil and rice vinegar and bring to a boil.
4. Add the eggs into the boiling broth without breaking the yolks and poach for about 1 minute.
5. Scatter the bok choy into the soup and allow it to cook for 1 minute.
6. Sprinkle with the scallion and serve with one egg in each bowl.

Healthy Pork Congee

Prep Time: 20 minutes, Cook Time: 1½ hours, Serves: 4

INGREDIENTS:

¾ cup jasmine rice, rinsed and drained
6 ounces (170 g) ground pork
2 garlic cloves, minced
10 cups water
2 tbsps. vegetable oil
1 tbsp. light soy sauce,
plus more for serving
2 tsps. peeled minced fresh ginger
2 tsps. Shaoxing rice wine
2 tsps. cornstarch
1 tsp. kosher salt

DIRECTIONS:

1. In a heavy-bottomed pot over high heat, bring the water to a boil. Stir in the salt and rice and reduce the heat to a simmer. Cover and cook, stirring frequently, for about 1½ hours, until the rice has turned to a soft porridge-like consistency.
2. While the congee is cooking, stir together the garlic, ginger, light soy, rice wine, and cornstarch in a medium bowl. Add the pork and let it marinate for about 15 minutes.
3. Heat a wok over high heat until a drop of water sizzles and evaporates on contact. Add the vegetable oil and swirl to coat the base of the wok evenly. Place the pork and stir-fry, tossing and breaking up the meat, for about 2 minutes. To get some caramelization, cook for another 1 to 2 minutes without stirring.
4. Top the congee with the stir-fried pork and serve hot.

Sizzling Rice and Shrimp Soup

Prep Time: 20 minutes, Cook Time: 15 minutes, Serves: 4

INGREDIENTS:

10 to 12 medium shrimp, peeled and deveined
1 cup cooked rice
2 baby bok choy heads, chopped into bite-size pieces
4 fresh shiitake mushrooms, stems removed and caps thinly sliced
1 large carrot, peeled and cut into ¼-inch-thick slices
4 cups low-sodium chicken broth
3 cups vegetable oil
2 tsps. sesame oil
2 tsps. light soy sauce
1 tsp. Shaoxing rice wine

DIRECTIONS:

1. Preheat the oven to 300ºF (150ºC). Line a baking sheet with aluminum foil. Spread the rice evenly and bake for about 15 to 20 minutes, until it feels dry. Keep aside to cool.
2. In a soup pot over high heat, bring the chicken broth to a boil. Reduce the heat to medium-high, add the mushrooms and carrot. Pour the light soy, sesame oil and rice wine into the soup and simmer for about 5 minutes.
3. Place the bok choy and bring to a boil over high heat. Turn the heat down to simmer and arrange the shrimp. Stir to distribute the vegetables and shrimp evenly and simmer over low heat while you fry the rice.
4. Add the oil in the wok and the oil should be about 1 to 1½ inches deep. Bring the oil over medium-high heat to 375ºF (190ºC). Dip the end of a wooden spoon into the oil. If the oil bubbles and sizzles around it, the oil is ready.
5. Fry the rice a scoopful at a time, until golden brown and crispy, for about 2 to 3 minutes. Lift the rice in clumps out of the oil and transfer to a paper towel–lined plate with a wire skimmer.
6. When ready to serve, distribute the soup and vegetables among 4 soup bowls. Place the crispy rice on top of each bowl and serve while still sizzling.

Hot and Sour Beef and Carrot Soup

Prep Time: 15 minutes, Cook Time: 8 minutes, Serves: 4

INGREDIENTS:

1 pound (454 g) shaved steak
1 medium carrot, julienned
1 medium onion, cut into 1-inch pieces
1 cup chopped bok choy
4 ounces (113 g) mushrooms, sliced
¼ cup rice vinegar
3 quarts vegetable or meat broth
2 garlic cloves, crushed and chopped
2 tbsps. cooking oil
1 tbsp. crushed chopped ginger
1 tsp. hot sesame oil

DIRECTIONS:

1. In a wok, heat the cooking oil over high heat until it shimmers.
2. Add the garlic, ginger and carrot and stir-fry for about 30 seconds.
3. Then place the onion and mushrooms and stir-fry for about 30 seconds.
4. Pour in the broth, sesame oil and rice vinegar and bring to a boil.
5. Put the bok choy and steak and stir for about 30 seconds.
6. Serve hot.

Hot-Sour Seafood and Vegetables Soup

Prep Time: 15 minutes, Cook Time: 8 minutes, Serves: 4

INGREDIENTS:

¼ pound (113 g) medium shrimp, shelled and deveined
¼ pound (113 g) sea scallops, cut in half widthwise
¼ pound (113 g) white fish (like cod or haddock), cut into 1-inch pieces
¼ pound (113 g) ground pork
1 cup chopped bok choy
4 scallions, cut into ½-inch pieces
½ cup julienned carrots
3 quarts vegetable, fish, or meat broth
¼ cup rice vinegar
2 garlic cloves, crushed and chopped
2 tbsps. cornstarch
1 tbsp. cooking oil
1 tbsp. hot sesame oil
1 tbsp. ginger, crushed and chopped

DIRECTIONS:

1. Whisk together the broth, sesame oil, rice vinegar and cornstarch in a large bowl. Set aside.
2. In a wok, heat the cooking oil over high heat until it shimmers.
3. Add the ginger, garlic and pork and stir-fry for about 1 minute.
4. Place the carrots and stir-fry for about 1 minute.
5. Pour the broth mixture to the wok and stir until the cornstarch dissolves entirely and the broth comes to a boil.
6. Then put the bok choy and allow to cook for about 1 minute.
7. Toss the shrimp, followed by the scallops and fish. Cook for about 2 minutes.
8. Garnish with the scallions and serve warm.

Healthy Pork and Egg Drop Soup

Prep Time: 15 minutes, Cook Time: 8 minutes, Serves: 4

INGREDIENTS:

1 pound (454 g) ground pork
4 eggs, beaten
1 cup chopped bok choy
1 ounce (28 g) dried, sliced shiitake or tree ear mushrooms
¼ cup cornstarch
4 scallions, cut into ½-inch pieces
2 garlic cloves, crushed and chopped
3 quarts plus 1¼ cups vegetable or meat broth, divided
1 tbsp. ginger, crushed and chopped

DIRECTIONS:

1. Mix 1 cup of the broth with the cornstarch and stir to form a slurry. Keep aside.
2. In a wok, boil ¼ cup of the broth over high heat.
3. Add the pork, garlic and ginger and cook for about 1 minute.
4. Pour the remaining 3 quarts broth and the mushrooms to the wok. Bring to a boil.
5. Toss the cornstarch slurry into the boiling broth until the broth thickens.
6. Stir the broth in one direction while drizzling the beaten eggs into the wok.
7. Add the bok choy to the broth and let cook for about 30 seconds.
8. Squeeze the scallions to bruise them, while sprinkling them into the soup.
9. Serve hot.

Chicken and Walnut Pomegranate Stew

Prep Time: 15 minutes, Cook Time: 2 hours, Serves: 6

INGREDIENTS:
1 (½-pound / 227-g) chicken legs, cut up
½ pound (227 g) walnuts, toasted and finely ground in a food processor
1 white onion, thinly sliced
4 cups pomegranate juice
2 tbsps. olive oil
2 tbsps. sugar (optional)
½ tsp. cardamom (optional)
1 tsp. salt

DIRECTIONS:
1. In a wok over high heat, heat the olive oil.
2. Fry onions and chicken for about 20 minutes.
3. Place cardamom, walnut purée, pomegranate juice and salt.
4. Heat until boiling. Lower the heat and cover the wok. Allow everything to simmer for 1½ hours.
5. Put some sugar and simmer for 30 more minutes.
6. Serve warm and enjoy.

Chicken and Vegetables Stir-Fry Soup

Prep Time: 15 minutes, Cook Time: 6 minutes, Serves: 4

INGREDIENTS:
1 pound (454 g) ground or finely chopped chicken
1 cup chopped bok choy
1 medium onion, diced
1 bell pepper (any color), cut into ½-inch pieces
3 quarts meat or vegetable broth
2 garlic cloves, crushed and chopped
4 scallions, cut into ¼-inch pieces
2 tbsps. cooking oil
1 tbsp. ginger, crushed and chopped
Fresh chopped herbs such as cilantro, mint, parsley, or basil, for garnish

DIRECTIONS:
1. In a wok, heat the cooking oil over high heat until it shimmers.
2. Add the garlic, ginger, chicken, onion, and bell pepper and stir-fry for about 1 minute.
3. Place the bok choy and stir-fry for about 30 seconds.
4. Pour the broth and bring to a gentle boil.
5. Squeeze the scallions to bruise them, while sprinkling them into the soup.
6. Garnish with chopped herbs and serve.

Malay Whole Chicken Curry, page 60

Curry Chicken, Carrot and Zucchini, page 60

Yellow Curry Chicken with Cauliflower, page 60

Chicken with Chipotle Gravy, page 54

52   Chapter 10 Poultry

Chapter 10 Poultry

Mexican Stir Fry Chicken and Black Beans

Prep Time: 20 minutes, Cook Time: 15 minutes, Serves: 4

INGREDIENTS:
1 pound (454 g) skinless, boneless chicken breast halves, diced
1 (15-ounce / 425-g) can black beans, rinsed and drained
1 cup shredded Cheddar cheese
1 green bell pepper, chopped
1 red bell pepper, chopped
½ cup prepared salsa
1 (1-ounce / 28-g) packet taco seasoning mix
2 tbsps. all-purpose flour, or as needed
3 tsps. olive oil, divided

DIRECTIONS:
1. In a wok over high heat, heat 1 tsp. olive oil. Fry red and green peppers for 5 minutes, then remove them.
2. Combine the taco seasoning and flour in a bowl. Place your chicken and coat the chicken evenly.
3. In the wok over high heat, heat the remaining 2 tsps. of olive oil. Fry chicken for 5 minutes, until cooked fully.
4. Mix the peppers from earlier with the chicken, then place some salsa and black beans.
5. Stir fry the chicken, beans, peppers and salsa for about 5 minutes.
6. Sprinkle with Cheddar cheese.
7. Enjoy.

East-Indian Chicken with Apricot Preserves

Prep Time: 15 minutes, Cook Time: 20 minutes, Serves: 4

INGREDIENTS:
1 pound (454 g) chicken tenders, cut into bite-size pieces
1 cup apricot preserves
1½ cups chicken stock
½ yellow onion, finely diced
¼ cup white vinegar
2 tbsps. olive oil
1 tbsp. butter
2 tsps. garam masala
1 tsp. hot pepper sauce
1 tsp. garlic powder
1 tsp. lime zest
Salt and black pepper to taste

DIRECTIONS:
1. Season the chicken with the garlic powder, garam masala, salt and pepper.
2. In a wok over medium heat, heat the olive oil and cook the onions for 5 minutes.
3. Place the chicken and cook for 5 minutes.
4. Take the chicken mixture into a bowl and set aside.
5. In the same wok, pour in 1 cup of the chicken stock and bring to a simmer, scraping the brown bits from the bottom of the wok with a scoop.
6. Stir in the vinegar, apricot preserves, remaining chicken stock and hot sauce.
7. Return the chicken mixture and simmer for 10 minutes.
8. Toss in the lime zest and butter just before serving.

Pad Thai Chicken and Rice Noodles

Prep Time: 15 minutes, Cook Time: 6 minutes, Serves: 4

INGREDIENTS:
1 pound (454 g) boneless chicken thighs, cut into 1-inch pieces
1 pound (454 g) cooked rice noodles
2 eggs, beaten
1 cup bean sprouts
½ cup chopped peanuts
2 bird's eye chiles, sliced into ¼-inch circles
2 garlic cloves, crushed and chopped
2 tbsps. cooking oil
2 tbsps. tamarind paste
2 tbsps. brown sugar
1 tbsp. fish sauce
1 tbsp. soy sauce
1 tbsp. cornstarch
1 tbsp. ginger, crushed and chopped
Coarsely chopped cilantro
Lime wedges

DIRECTIONS:
1. Whisk together the tamarind paste, soy sauce, fish sauce, brown sugar and cornstarch in a small bowl. Keep aside.
2. In a wok, heat the cooking oil over high heat until it shimmers.
3. Add the garlic, ginger and eggs and stir-fry for about 1 minute.
4. Place the chicken and bird's eye chiles and stir-fry for about 1 minute.
5. Toss the tamarind paste mixture and stir until a glaze is formed.
6. Garnish with the peanuts, bean sprouts, cilantro and lime wedges. Serve over the noodles.

Sesame Honey Chicken

Prep Time: 15 minutes, Cook Time: 5 minutes, Serves: 4 to 6

INGREDIENTS:
MARINADE:
2 (5-ounce / 142-g) boneless chicken breast halves
1 egg white
3 tsps. cornstarch
½ tsp. salt
Pinch ground white pepper
SAUCE:
2 tbsps. honey
½ tsp. sesame oil
1½ tbsps. apple cider vinegar
1 tsp. soy sauce
½ tsp. salt
STIR-FRY:
1 scallion, chopped
2 tbsps. peanut oil
1 tsp. toasted sesame seeds

DIRECTIONS:
1. Add the egg white, cornstarch, salt and pepper over the chicken and toss to combine well. Marinate at room temperature for about 20 minutes.
2. Prepare the sauce by mixing together the honey, apple cider vinegar, soy sauce, sesame oil and salt in a small bowl.
3. In a wok, heat the peanut oil over medium-high heat.
4. Place the chicken and stir-fry until completely cooked.
5. Stir in the sauce, mixing to coat the chicken evenly.
6. Scatter the sesame seeds over the chicken, stirring well.
7. Take to a serving dish and sprinkle with the scallion. Serve warm.

Chicken with Chipotle Gravy

Prep Time: 5 minutes, Cook Time: 10 minutes, Serves: 2

INGREDIENTS:
2 skinless, boneless chicken breast halves
¾ cup chicken broth
2 tbsps. minced green onions
2 tbsps. butter
1 tbsp. olive oil
1 tbsp. all-purpose flour
½ tsp. chipotle chili powder, or more to taste
Salt and fresh ground pepper to taste

DIRECTIONS:
1. Use a meat mallet to pound the chicken breast halves into ½-inch thickness by placing it between 2 heavy plastic sheets.
2. In a wok over high heat, heat the oil until it begins to simmer.
3. Turn the heat to medium and place the chicken breasts and season with salt and black pepper.
4. Cook the chicken for 5 minutes on both sides or until browned.
5. Put the breasts into a plate covered with foil to make them warm.
6. In the same wok over high heat, melt the butter and cook the flour stirring from time to time for 2 minutes.
7. Pour in the broth and cook for about 1 to 2 minutes, scraping the brown bits.
8. Stir in the chicken, green onion and chipotle powder and cook for 1 to 2 minutes.
9. Serve warm.

Cheesy Chipotle Chicken Sandwich

Prep Time: 15 minutes, Cook Time: 30 minutes, Serves: 4

INGREDIENTS:
4 skinless, boneless chicken breast halves
8 slices sourdough bread
1 cup torn lettuce
⅓ cup light mayonnaise
4 slices Mozzarella cheese
1 green onion, chopped
1 clove garlic, minced
1½ tbsps. chopped green onion
1½ tbsps. sweet pickle relish
1 tbsp. red wine vinegar
1 tbsp. canned chipotle peppers in adobo sauce, seeded and minced
1 tbsp. fresh lime juice
2 tsps. olive oil
½ tsp. dried oregano
½ tsp. white sugar
Salt and ground black pepper to taste

DIRECTIONS:
1. In a large wok over medium heat, heat the oil and sear the chicken breasts for 10 minutes per side or until browned.
2. Stir in 1 tsp. lime juice, vinegar, green onion, garlic, sugar, oregano, salt and black pepper and cook for 5 minutes per side.
3. Take the chicken mixture to a plate and cover with a piece of foil to keep warm.
4. In a blender, place the mayonnaise and chipotle pepper and pulse until smooth.
5. Mix together chipotle mayonnaise, sweet pickle relish and remaining green onion in a bowl.
6. Toast the slices of bread.
7. Evenly spread the chipotle-mayonnaise mixture over 4 bread slices.
8. Distribute the lettuce over the remaining 4 bread slices evenly, followed by 1 chicken breast and 1 cheese slice.
9. Cover with the slices of mayonnaise to make a sandwich and serve hot.

Honey Chicken

Prep Time: 15 minutes, Cook Time: 6 minutes, Serves: 4

INGREDIENTS:
1 pound (454 g) boneless chicken thighs, cut into 1-inch pieces
1 medium carrot, roll-cut into ½-inch pieces
1 medium onion, cut into 1-inch pieces
1 medium red bell pepper, cut into 1-inch pieces
¼ cup honey
4 scallions, cut into 1-inch pieces
3 garlic cloves, crushed and chopped
2 tbsps. cooking oil
2 tbsps. soy sauce
2 tbsps. rice wine
1 tbsp. Chinese five-spice powder
1 tbsp. cornstarch
1 tbsp. ginger, crushed and chopped
1 tsp. hot sesame oil

DIRECTIONS:
1. In a large bowl or resealable plastic bag, combine the soy sauce, honey, rice wine, and five-spice powder. Place the chicken and keep aside to marinate.
2. In a wok, heat the cooking oil over high heat until it shimmers.
3. Add the carrot, garlic, and ginger and stir-fry for about 1 minute.
4. Place the chicken, reserving the marinade, to the wok and stir-fry for about 1 minute.
5. Then put the onion and bell pepper and stir-fry for about 1 minute.
6. Pour the reserved marinade and the cornstarch and stir until a light glaze forms.
7. Toss the sesame oil and stir-fry for about 30 seconds.
8. Garnish with the scallions. Serve hot.

Classic General Tso's Chicken

Prep Time: 25 minutes, Cook Time: 10 minutes, Serves: 4 to 6

INGREDIENTS:
MARINADE:
2 boneless chicken breast halves, cut into bite-size pieces
2 tsps. cornstarch
¼ tsp. salt
2 pinches ground white pepper
SAUCE:
2 tbsps. ketchup
3 tsps. rice vinegar
2 tsps. soy sauce
2 tsps. brown sugar
2 tsps. hoisin sauce
STIR-FRY:
1 scallion, chopped
¼ dried red chile
2 tbsps. peanut oil
½ tsp. toasted sesame seeds

DIRECTIONS:
1. Mix the cornstarch, salt, and white pepper in a small bowl. Sprinkle over the chicken, tossing to coat well, and marinate at room temperature for about 20 minutes.
2. At the same time, make the sauce by combining the ketchup, hoisin sauce, rice vinegar, brown sugar and soy sauce in a separate small bowl, mixing it well. Keep the sauce aside.
3. In a wok, heat the peanut oil over medium-high heat.
4. Place the chicken and stir-fry in batches until completely cooked and slightly brown.
5. Put the chile and pour in the sauce. Stir to evenly coat the chicken in the sauce.
6. Remove from the heat and take the dish to a serving plate.
7. Sprinkle with the sesame seeds and chopped scallion. Serve hot.

Chicken with Asparagus

Prep Time: 25 minutes, Cook Time: 5 minutes, Serves: 4 to 6

INGREDIENTS:
MARINADE:
2 (5-ounce / 142-g) boneless skinless chicken breast halves, cut into bite-size pieces
2 tsps. Shaoxing wine
3 tsps. cornstarch
½ tsp. salt
Pinch freshly ground black pepper
SAUCE:
1 tsp. rice vinegar
1 tbsp. oyster sauce
½ tsp. dark soy sauce
½ tsp. soy sauce
1 tsp. freshly ground black pepper
STIR-FRY:
½ pound (227 g) asparagus (about ½ bunch), stems trimmed, cut into 1-inch pieces
2 tbsps. peanut oil

DIRECTIONS:
1. In a large bowl, add the Shaoxing wine, cornstarch, salt and pepper over the chicken and toss to combine well. Marinate at room temperature for about 20 minutes.
2. Prepare the sauce by combining the oyster sauce, rice vinegar, dark soy sauce, soy sauce and pepper in a small bowl and mix it well. Keep it aside.
3. In a wok, heat the peanut oil over medium-high heat.
4. Place the chicken and stir-fry until the chicken is half cooked.
5. Put the asparagus and stir-fry until it looks bright green and the chicken is completely cooked, or for 2 minutes.
6. Add the sauce to the wok, and stir to combine all the ingredients well.
7. Transfer to a serving dish and serve warm.

Coconut Chicken Thigh

Prep Time: 15 minutes, Cook Time: 6 minutes, Serves: 4

INGREDIENTS:
- 1 pound (454 g) boneless chicken thighs, cut into 1-inch pieces
- 1 medium red onion, cut into 1-inch pieces
- 2 cups sugar snap or snow pea pods
- 2 garlic cloves, crushed and chopped
- ½ cup chopped cilantro or parsley
- ¼ cup canned coconut milk
- 2 tbsps. coconut oil
- 2 tbsps. fish sauce
- 2 tbsps. lime juice
- 1 tbsp. cornstarch
- 1 tbsp. ginger, crushed and chopped
- 1 tsp. hot sesame oil

DIRECTIONS:
1. Whisk together the coconut milk, fish sauce, lime juice, sesame oil and cornstarch in a small bowl. Set aside.
2. In a wok, heat the coconut oil over high heat until it shimmers.
3. Add the garlic, ginger and chicken and stir-fry for about 1 minute.
4. Put the onion and pea pods and stir-fry for about 1 minute.
5. Pour the coconut milk mixture to the wok and stir until a glaze forms.
6. Sprinkle with the chopped cilantro or parsley and serve warm.

Ginger Chicken in Peanut Oil

Prep Time: 25 minutes, Cook Time: 5 minutes, Serves: 4 to 6

INGREDIENTS:

MARINADE:
- 2 chicken breast halves, cut into bite-size pieces
- 1 tbsp. cornstarch
- 1 tsp. sesame oil
- ½ tsp. salt
- Pinch ground white pepper

STIR-FRY:
- 2 bunches scallions, cut into 1-inch pieces
- 2-inch piece ginger, peeled and thinly sliced
- 2 tbsps. water
- 2 tbsps. peanut oil
- 1 tbsp. sesame oil
- 1 tsp. soy sauce

DIRECTIONS:
1. Add 1 tsp. of sesame oil, cornstarch, salt and pepper over the chicken and toss to coat well. Marinate at room temperature for 20 minutes.
2. In a wok, heat the peanut oil over medium-high heat.
3. Place the chicken and stir-fry in two batches until completely cooked.
4. Take the chicken from the wok and keep aside.
5. Pour the remaining 1 tbsp. of sesame oil to the wok. Put the ginger and stir-fry for 1 minute.
6. Take the chicken back to the wok and pour in the water and soy sauce. Stir-fry until the sauce thickens a little.
7. Place the scallions, stir to combine well, then remove from the heat. Serve warm.

Orange Chicken and Sugar Snap

Prep Time: 15 minutes, Cook Time: 8 minutes, Serves: 4

INGREDIENTS:
- 1 pound (454 g) boneless chicken thighs, cut into 1-inch pieces
- 2 cups sugar snap or snow pea pods
- 1 medium red bell pepper, cut into 1-inch pieces
- 1 medium onion, cut into 1-inch pieces
- 4 scallions, cut into 1-inch pieces
- 2 garlic cloves, crushed and chopped
- ¼ cup plus 2 tbsps. cornstarch, divided
- ¼ cup orange juice
- Zest of 1 orange
- ¼ cup cooking oil
- 2 tbsps. rice vinegar
- 2 tbsps. rice wine
- 2 tbsps. brown sugar
- 2 tbsps. soy sauce
- 1 tbsp. ginger, crushed and chopped
- 1 tsp. hot sesame oil

DIRECTIONS:
1. Whisk together the orange zest, sesame oil, 2 tbsps. of the cornstarch, the orange juice, rice vinegar, rice wine, brown sugar and soy sauce in a small bowl. Keep aside.
2. Toss the remaining ¼ cup of cornstarch in a resealable plastic bag or covered bowl. Coat the chicken with the cornstarch, ensuring the pieces are evenly coated.
3. In a wok, heat the cooking oil over high heat until it shimmers.
4. Add the garlic and ginger and stir-fry for about 30 seconds.
5. Shallow-fry the chicken for about 3 to 4 minutes until lightly browned.
6. Remove the chicken and keep aside. Remove and discard all but 2 tbsps. of oil from the wok.
7. Add the onion to the wok and stir-fry for about 1 minute.
8. Put the pea pods and bell pepper and stir-fry for about 30 seconds.
9. Pour in the orange juice mixture and stir until a glaze forms.
10. Take the chicken to the wok. Toss and sprinkle with the scallions. Serve warm.

Chapter 10 Poultry

Stir-Fried Chicken and Mushroom

Prep Time: 15 minutes, Cook Time: 6 minutes, Serves: 4

INGREDIENTS:

1 pound (454 g) boneless chicken thighs, cut into 1-inch pieces
2 cups sugar snap or snow pea pods
4 ounces (113 g) sliced mushrooms
1 medium red bell pepper, cut into ½-inch pieces
4 scallions, cut into 1-inch pieces
2 cloves garlic, crushed and chopped
2 tbsps. cooking oil
2 tbsps. sugar
2 tbsps. soy sauce
2 tbsps. rice wine
2 tbsps. rice vinegar
1 tbsp. cornstarch
1 tbsp. ginger, crushed and chopped

DIRECTIONS:

1. Whisk together the soy sauce, rice wine, rice vinegar, sugar and cornstarch in a small bowl. Set aside.
2. In a wok, heat the cooking oil over high heat until it shimmers.
3. Add the garlic, ginger, and chicken and stir-fry for about 1 minute.
4. Add the mushrooms, pea pods and bell pepper and stir-fry for about 1 minute.
5. Stir the soy sauce mixture into the wok and stir until a light glaze forms.
6. Sprinkle with the scallions and serve hot.

Cilantro-Lime Chicken and Pineapple

Prep Time: 15 minutes, Cook Time: 6 minutes, Serves: 4

INGREDIENTS:

1 pound (454 g) boneless chicken thighs, cut into 1-inch pieces
1 (8-ounce / 227-g) can of pineapple chunks, drained, juice reserved
2 cups sugar snap or snow pea pods
1 medium onion, cut into 1-inch pieces
1 medium red bell pepper, cut into 1-inch pieces
1 cup chopped cilantro
2 garlic cloves, crushed and chopped
Zest and juice of 1 lime
2 tbsps. cooking oil
2 tbsps. fish sauce
1 tbsp. cornstarch
1 tbsp. ginger, crushed and chopped

DIRECTIONS:

1. Whisk together the pineapple juice, lime zest and juice, fish sauce and cornstarch in a small bowl. Set aside.
2. In a wok, heat the cooking oil over high heat until it shimmers.
3. Add the garlic, ginger and chicken and stir-fry for about 1 minute.
4. Place the onion and stir-fry for about 1 minute.
5. Then put the pea pods and bell pepper and stir-fry for about 1 minute.
6. Take the pineapple chunks to the wok and stir-fry for about 1 minute.
7. Pour the pineapple and lime juice mixture to the wok and stir until a light glaze forms.
8. Sprinkle with the cilantro and serve warm.

Sweet and Sour Pineapple and Chicken

Prep Time: 15 minutes, Cook Time: 8 minutes, Serves: 4

INGREDIENTS:

1 pound (454 g) boneless chicken thighs, cut into 1-inch pieces
1 (8-ounce / 227-g) can pineapple chunks, drained, juice reserved
2 cups sugar snap or snow pea pods
1 medium red bell pepper, cut into 1-inch pieces
4 scallions, cut into 1-inch pieces
2 garlic cloves, crushed and chopped
¼ cup cooking oil
¼ cup plus 2 tbsps. cornstarch, divided
¼ cup rice vinegar
2 tbsps. ketchup
1 tbsp. ginger, crushed and chopped

DIRECTIONS:

1. Whisk together the rice vinegar, ketchup, pineapple juice, and 2 tbsps. of the cornstarch in a small bowl. Set aside.
2. Toss the remaining ¼ cup of cornstarch in a resealable plastic bag or covered bowl. Coat the chicken with the cornstarch and set aside.
3. In a wok over high heat, heat the cooking oil until it shimmers.
4. Add the garlic and ginger and stir-fry for about 30 seconds to lightly brown.
5. Place the chicken and shallow-fry for about 3 to 4 minutes until lightly browned.
6. Take the chicken from the wok and set aside.
7. Remove and discard all but 2 tbsps. of oil from the wok.
8. Place the pea pods and bell pepper and stir-fry for about 30 seconds.
9. Put the pineapple chunks and stir-fry for about 30 seconds.
10. Pour the rice vinegar mixture and stir until a glaze forms.
11. Take the chicken back to the wok, toss with the other ingredients and garnish with the scallions. Serve hot.

Lemongrass Chicken and Bok Choy

Prep Time: 15 minutes, Cook Time: 6 minutes, Serves: 4

INGREDIENTS:

1 pound (454 g) boneless chicken thighs, cut into 1-inch pieces
2 heads baby bok choy, leaves separated
1 medium red onion, cut into 1-inch pieces
4 ounces (113 g) sliced mushrooms
1 medium red bell pepper, cut into 1-inch pieces
2 lemongrass hearts (the bottom 2 inches of the white inner layers), finely minced
2 garlic cloves, crushed and chopped
2 tbsps. cooking oil
1 tbsp. ginger, crushed and chopped
1 tsp. hot sesame oil
1 tsp. fish sauce
Fresh chopped herbs, such as cilantro, mint, or parsley, for garnish

DIRECTIONS:

1. In a wok, heat the cooking oil over high heat until it shimmers.
2. Add the garlic, ginger, lemongrass, and chicken and stir-fry for about 1 minute.
3. Place the onion, mushrooms and bell pepper stir-fry for about 1 minute.
4. Toss the bok choy, sesame oil and fish sauce and stir-fry for about 30 seconds.
5. Sprinkle with chopped herbs of your choice and serve warm.

West African Chicken and Tomato Rice

Prep Time: 30 minutes, Cook Time: 1 hour, Serves: 6

INGREDIENTS:

3 pounds (1.4 kg) chicken pieces
16 ounces (454 g) canned tomatoes, cut up
1 cup long grain rice
1 medium onion, chopped
1¼ cups chicken broth
2 tbsps. oil
1 tbsp. parsley, chopped
1 bay leaf
½ tsp. thyme, crushed
½ tsp. ground ginger
½ tsp. cinnamon
½ tsp. salt
¼ tsp. ground red pepper

DIRECTIONS:

1. In a wok over medium heat, heat the oil. Cook the chicken pieces for about 6 to 7 minutes on each side.
2. Drain the chicken pieces and set aside.
3. Stir the onion into the remaining oil in the wok. Cook for about 4 minutes. Drain the onion and discard the remaining oil.
4. Take the chicken back with onion into wok with broth, undrained tomatoes, and seasonings.
5. Let them cook until they start boiling. Reduce the heat to low and cover the lid. Allow the stew to cook for about 32 minutes.
6. Discard the fat that rise on top. Toss the rice into the wok. Cover the lid and let them cook for about 32 minutes.
7. Once the time is up, drain the bay leaf and discard.
8. Sprinkle with some parsley then serve warm.

Chicken with Bamboo Shoots and Mushrooms

Prep Time: 25 minutes, Cook Time: 5 minutes, Serves: 6 to 8

INGREDIENTS:
MARINADE:
2 boneless chicken breast halves, cut into thin strips
3 tbsps. cornstarch
2 tsps. soy sauce
2 pinches ground white pepper
SAUCE:
½ cup chicken stock
1 tsp. Shaoxing wine
1 tsp. cornstarch
1 tsp. rice vinegar
½ tsp. sugar
½ tsp. salt
STIR-FRY:
2 tbsps. peanut oil
2 cups snow peas
¼ cup bamboo shoots
¼ cup water chestnuts, sliced
4 to 6 button mushrooms, sliced
1-inch piece ginger, peeled and julienned
2 garlic cloves, minced

DIRECTIONS:

1. Pour the soy sauce, cornstarch and pepper over the chicken then toss to coat well. Marinate at room temperature for about 20 minutes.
2. Prepare the sauce by mixing together the chicken stock, rice vinegar, Shaoxing wine, cornstarch, salt and sugar in a separate bowl. Keep aside.
3. In a wok, heat the peanut oil over medium-high heat. Place the chicken to the wok and stir-fry until almost completely cooked. Take the chicken from the wok and keep it aside.
4. Stir-fry the garlic and ginger for 15 seconds and place the snow peas.
5. When the snow peas start to turn bright green after 2 minutes, stir in the bamboo shoots, mushrooms and water chestnuts.
6. When the mushrooms begin to soften, pour in the sauce and take the chicken back to the wok. Stir-fry to combine all the ingredients well.
7. When the sauce has thickened for about 20 seconds, take the dish to a serving plate. Serve warm.

Sesame Oil Ginger Chicken

Prep Time: 5 minutes, Cook Time: 10 minutes, Serves: 4 to 6

INGREDIENTS:
- 4 chicken drumsticks (bone-in), chopped into 2 or 3 pieces each
- ½ cup water
- 2-inch piece ginger, peeled and julienned
- 2 tbsps. Shaoxing wine
- 2 tbsps. sesame oil
- 2 tsps. soy sauce
- ¼ tsp. dark soy sauce
- Pinch ground white pepper

DIRECTIONS:
1. In a wok, heat the sesame oil over medium-high heat.
2. Place the ginger and stir-fry until it turns a very light golden brown.
3. Put the chicken pieces and stir-fry for 1 minute to cook the surface.
4. Toss in the Shaoxing wine, dark soy sauce, soy sauce, water and pepper.
5. Stir the chicken well, turn the heat to low and simmer for about 5 to 10 minutes until tender.
6. Take to a serving plate and serve hot.

Chicken Stir Fry with Peanut Butter

Prep Time: 15 minutes, Cook Time: 15 minutes, Serves: 4

INGREDIENTS:
- 1 (9-ounce / 225-g) package diced cooked chicken breast meat
- 1 (12-ounce / 340-g) package shredded coleslaw mix
- 3 cups bean sprouts
- 2 cups sliced mushrooms
- 1 small head broccoli, cut into spears
- ½ sweet onion, sliced
- ½ cup chicken broth
- ¼ cup creamy peanut butter
- 1 tbsp. tamari or soy sauce
- 1 pinch red pepper flakes (optional)

DIRECTIONS:
1. In a large wok over medium heat, bring the broth a boil.
2. Toss in the broccoli, onion and mushroom. Cover the lid and cook for about 6 minutes. Add the peanut butter, tamari and pepper flakes. Combine them until they become smooth.
3. Stir in the bean sprouts, coleslaw mix and chicken. Cook for about 4 minutes. Serve hot.

Chicken and Bacon Rice

Prep Time: 10 minutes, Cook Time: 45 minutes, Serves: 8

INGREDIENTS:
- 1 whole chicken, cut up pieces
- 2 cups long-grain rice
- 12 ounces (340 g) bacon, chopped
- 4 stalks celery, cut into 1 inch pieces
- 1 carrot, cut in 1 inch pieces
- 4 cups chicken broth, boiling
- 2 tbsps. fresh parsley, chopped
- 1 bay leaf
- Salt and pepper

DIRECTIONS:
1. In a large wok over very low heat, cook the bacon until crisp.
2. Take the bacon to a paper towel lined plate to drain and then crumble it.
3. Drain the grease, leaving 2 tbsps. inside the wok.
4. In the same wok, add the rice and cook gently until browned lightly.
5. Toss the boiling stock and bring back to a boil.
6. Stir in the bay leaf, chicken, vegetables, salt and pepper.
7. Turn the heat and simmer, covered for 30 minutes.
8. Sprinkle with the crumbled bacon and parsley. Serve warm.

Kadai Chicken with Yogurt

Prep Time: 15 minutes, Cook Time: 8 minutes, Serves: 4

INGREDIENTS:
- 1 pound (454 g) boneless chicken thighs, cut into 1-inch pieces
- ½ cup whole-milk Greek yogurt
- 1 medium carrot, roll-cut into ½-inch pieces
- 1 medium onion, cut into 1-inch pieces
- 2 chiles, sliced into ¼-inch circles (no need to core or seed them)
- 2 garlic cloves, crushed and chopped
- 2 tbsps. ghee
- 1 tbsp. ginger, crushed and chopped
- 1 tsp. ground coriander
- 1 tsp. paprika
- 1 tsp. cumin

DIRECTIONS:
1. In a wok, heat the ghee over high heat until it shimmers.
2. Add the garlic, ginger, carrot and chicken and stir-fry for about 1 minute.
3. Place the onion, cumin, coriander and paprika and stir-fry for about 1 minute.
4. Then put the sliced chiles and stir-fry for about 1 minute.
5. Remove from the heat and stir the yogurt into the wok. Serve hot.

Malay Whole Chicken Curry

Prep Time: 20 minutes, Cook Time: 35 minutes, Serves: 4

INGREDIENTS:

- 1 (2- to 3-pound / 907-g to 1.4-kg) whole chicken, bones and skin removed, cut into pieces
- 1 (14½-ounce / 411-g) can whole peeled tomatoes, drained
- 1 (14-ounce / 397-g) can unsweetened coconut milk
- 1 onion, chopped
- 2 cloves garlic, peeled and chopped
- 1 lemon, juiced
- 1 tbsp. olive oil
- 1 bay leaf
- 2 tsps. curry powder
- ⅛ tsp. salt

DIRECTIONS:

1. In a large, heavy wok on medium heat, heat the olive oil and cook the garlic, onion and bay leaf until browned lightly.
2. Toss in the curry powder, tomatoes, and salt and cook for 5 minutes.
3. Stir in the chicken and cook for 15 to 20 minutes.
4. Turn the heat to low.
5. Gently add the coconut milk, stirring from time to time during the period of 10 minutes.
6. Pour in the lemon juice and serve hot.

Garlic Chicken with Cashew Nuts

Prep Time: 5 minutes, Cook Time: 10 minutes, Serves: 4 to 6

INGREDIENTS:

- 2 boneless skinless chicken breast halves, cut into thin strips
- ½ cup cashews, lightly roasted
- ½ onion, thinly sliced
- 2 garlic cloves, minced
- 1 scallion, chopped
- 2 tbsps. peanut oil
- 1½ tbsps. brown sugar
- 1 tbsp. oyster sauce
- 1 tbsp. soy sauce
- 1 tsp. fish sauce

DIRECTIONS:

1. In a wok, heat the peanut oil over medium heat.
2. Add the onion and garlic and stir-fry until aromatic.
3. Place the chicken and stir-fry until the chicken is almost completely cooked.
4. Mix the brown sugar, oyster sauce, soy sauce and fish sauce, and pour into the chicken.
5. Increase the heat to high, stir to mix well, and continue stirring until the chicken is completely cooked.
6. Stir in the cashew nuts.
7. Sprinkle with the chopped scallion and serve warm.

Yellow Curry Chicken with Cauliflower

Prep Time: 15 minutes, Cook Time: 40 minutes, Serves: 4

INGREDIENTS:

- 1 pound (454 g) skinless, boneless chicken breast halves, chopped
- 1 (14-ounce / 397-g) can unsweetened coconut milk
- 1 small head cauliflower, chopped
- 1 white onion, chopped
- 2 cloves garlic, crushed
- ⅓ cup chicken stock
- 2½ tbsps. yellow curry powder
- 2 tbsps. vegetable oil
- 1 tsp. garlic salt
- Salt and pepper to taste

DIRECTIONS:

1. In a large wok over medium heat, heat the oil and cook the onion and garlic until soft.
2. Toss in the chicken and sauté for 10 minutes.
3. Stir in the cauliflower, garlic salt, curry powder, coconut milk, chicken stock, salt and pepper.
4. Turn the heat to low and simmer for 30 minutes, stirring from time to time. Serve warm.

Curry Chicken, Carrot and Zucchini

Prep Time: 10 minutes, Cook Time: 15 minutes, Serves: 4

INGREDIENTS:

- 1 pound (454 g) skinless, boneless chicken breast halves, cut into thin strips
- 1 (14-ounce / 397-g) can light coconut milk
- 1 cup sliced halved zucchini
- 1 onion, quartered then halved
- 1 red bell pepper, seeded and sliced into strips
- ½ cup sliced carrots
- 2 tbsps. chopped fresh cilantro
- 1 tbsp. cornstarch
- 1 tbsp. Thai red curry paste
- 2 tsps. olive oil

DIRECTIONS:

1. In a large wok on medium-high heat, heat the oil and sauté the chicken pieces for 3 minutes.
2. Stir in the curry paste, bell pepper, zucchini, carrot and onion and sauté for a few minutes.
3. In a bowl, dissolve the cornstarch entirely in the coconut milk.
4. Toss the cornstarch mixture in the curry and bring to a boil.
5. Turn the heat to medium heat and simmer for 1 minute.
6. Sprinkle with the cilantro and serve hot.

Chicken with Walnuts

Prep Time: 15 minutes, Cook Time: 40 minutes, Serves: 4

INGREDIENTS:
- 4 skinless, boneless chicken breast halves
- 1 bottle pomegranate paste or syrup
- 1 cup finely ground walnuts
- 1 onion, finely chopped
- 2 tbsps. olive oil

DIRECTIONS:
1. In a wok over high heat, heat the olive oil.
2. Fry the onions until tender.
3. Place chicken to the onions. Fry the chicken until brown on all the sides. Set aside.
4. Put walnuts to the oil and fry for about 10 minutes.
5. Arrange chicken onions with walnuts and add the pomegranate paste.
6. Turn the heat to low. Allow contents to simmer for about 20 minutes while covered. Stir occasionally.
7. Transfer to a plate and enjoy.

Garlic Kimchi Chicken and Cabbage

Prep Time: 10 minutes, Cook Time: 5 minutes, Serves: 4

INGREDIENTS:
- 1 pound (454 g) ground chicken
- 1 cup chopped kimchi
- 2 heads baby bok choy, leaves separated
- 2 garlic cloves, crushed and chopped
- 2 tbsps. cooking oil
- 2 tbsps. sesame seeds
- 1 tbsp. ginger, crushed and chopped
- 1 tbsp. fish sauce
- 1 tbsp. gochujang
- 1 tbsp. toasted sesame oil

DIRECTIONS:
1. In a wok, heat the cooking oil over high heat until it shimmers.
2. Add the garlic, ginger, and chicken and stir-fry for about 1 minute.
3. Put the kimchi, bok choy, gochujang and fish sauce and stir-fry for about 1 minute.
4. Pour in the sesame oil and sesame seeds and toss.
5. Serve hot.

Cambodian Chicken Basil Pesto

Prep Time: 10 minutes, Cook Time: 12 minutes, Serves: 2

INGREDIENTS:
- 2 cups chicken thighs, chopped
- 1 bunch basil leaves
- 1 handful peanuts
- ¾ cup water
- 4 hot chili peppers, chopped
- 2 tbsps. cooking oil
- 1 tbsp. chopped garlic
- 1 tbsp. fish sauce
- 1 tsp. oyster sauce
- 1 tsp. black sweet soy sauce

DIRECTIONS:
1. In a wok over high heat, heat the oil and cook the chicken, garlic, chilies, fish sauce and water for 10 minutes.
2. Stir in the basil, peanuts, oyster sauce and sweet soy sauce and cook for 2 minutes.
3. Enjoy warm.

Chicken and Vegetables with Hoisin Sauce

Prep Time: 10 minutes, Cook Time: 5 minutes, Serves: 4

INGREDIENTS:
- 1 pound (454 g) ground chicken
- 2 cups sugar snap or snow pea pods
- 1 medium carrot, roll-cut into ½-inch pieces
- 1 medium onion, cut into 1-inch pieces
- ¼ cup hoisin sauce
- 2 garlic cloves, crushed and chopped
- 2 tbsps. cooking oil
- 1 tbsp. ginger, crushed and chopped

DIRECTIONS:
1. In a wok, heat the cooking oil over high heat until it shimmers.
2. Add the garlic, ginger, carrot and chicken and stir-fry for about 1 minute.
3. Place the onion and pea pods and stir-fry for about 1 minute.
4. Toss the hoisin sauce and stir-fry for about 30 seconds.
5. Serve hot.

Orange Chicken with Sesame Seeds

Prep Time: 25 minutes, Cook Time: 5 minutes, Serves: 4 to 6

INGREDIENTS:
MARINADE:
2 tsps. soy sauce
2 (5-ounce / 142-g) boneless chicken breast halves, cut into bite-size pieces
3 tsps. cornstarch
2 pinches ground white pepper
SAUCE:
3 to 4 orange peel strips, julienned
2 tbsps. apple cider vinegar
2 star anise petals
1 clove
2 tbsps. water
1 tbsp. orange juice
2 tsps. brown sugar
2 tsps. cornstarch
1 tsp. soy sauce
½ tsp. ketchup
Pinch red pepper flakes
STIR-FRY:
1 scallion, chopped
2 tbsps. peanut oil
½ tsp. toasted sesame seeds

DIRECTIONS:
1. Sprinkle the chicken with the cornstarch, pepper and soy sauce and toss to combine well. Marinate at room temperature for about 20 minutes.
2. Make the sauce by mixing together the orange peel, water, apple cider vinegar, orange juice, cornstarch, brown sugar, soy sauce, ketchup, star anise, clove and red pepper flakes in a small bowl. Set it aside.
3. In a wok, heat the peanut oil over medium-high heat.
4. Place the chicken and stir-fry until slightly golden brown. Take the chicken from the wok and keep it aside.
5. Add the sauce into the wok and stir until it turns thick.
6. Take the chicken back to the wok and stir to coat each piece well.
7. Transfer to a serving plate and sprinkle with the scallion and sesame seeds.
8. Serve hot.

Pork with Bok Choy and Carrot, page 64

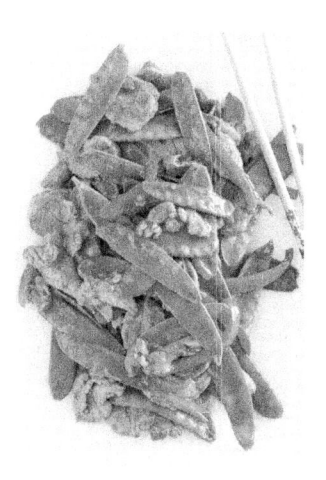

Hoisin Pork and Snow Peas Stir-Fry, page 64

Pork Ribs with Black Bean Sauce, page 68

Stir-Fried Ginger Lamb, page 66

Chapter 11 Pork, Beef and Lamb

Chapter 11 Pork, Beef and Lamb

Mexican Mac n Cheese with Beef

Prep Time: 10 minutes, Cook Time: 15 minutes, Serves: 6

INGREDIENTS:

1 pound (454 g) lean ground beef
1 (7.3 ounce / 207-g) package white Cheddar macaroni and cheese mix
¼ cup milk
1 (1¼-ounce / 35-g) package taco seasoning mix
2 tbsps. butter

DIRECTIONS:

1. In a large wok on medium heat, cook the beef until browned completely.
2. Drain the excess grease from the wok.
3. Place the taco seasoning and water according to seasoning package directions and simmer for 10 minutes.
4. Turn off the heat and set aside.
5. Prepare the macaroni and cheese according to package's directions, putting butter and milk as indicated.
6. Pour in the beef mixture and stir to combine well.
7. Serve hot.

Hoisin Pork and Snow Peas Stir-Fry

Prep Time: 15 minutes, Cook Time: 10 minutes, Serves: 4

INGREDIENTS:

¾ pound (340 g) boneless pork loin, thinly sliced into julienne strips
4 ounces (113 g) snow peas, thinly sliced on the diagonal
4 peeled fresh ginger slices, each about the size of a quarter
2 tbsps. vegetable oil
2 tbsps. hoisin sauce
1 tbsp. water
2 tsps. light soy sauce
2 tsps. Shaoxing rice wine
½ tsp. chili paste
Kosher salt

DIRECTIONS:

1. Stir together the rice wine, light soy and chili paste in a bowl. Add the pork and toss to coat well. Keep aside to marinate for about 10 minutes.
2. Heat a wok over high heat until a drop of water sizzles and evaporates on contact. Add the oil and swirl to coat the base of the wok well. Season the oil with the ginger and a pinch of salt. Let the ginger sizzle in the oil for 30 seconds, swirling slowly.
3. Add the pork and marinade and stir-fry for about 2 to 3 minutes, until no longer pink. Place the snow peas and stir-fry for 1 minute, until soft and translucent. Stir in the hoisin sauce and water to loosen the sauce. Continue to toss and flip for about 30 seconds, or until the sauce is heated through and the pork and snow peas are coated evenly.
4. Transfer the dish to a platter and serve warm.

Pork with Bok Choy and Carrot

Prep Time: 15 minutes, Cook Time: 10 minutes, Serves: 4

INGREDIENTS:

¾ pound (340 g) ground pork
2 to 3 heads bok choy, cut crosswise into bite-size pieces
1 carrot, peeled and julienned
Cooked rice, for serving
2 garlic cloves, peeled and slightly smashed
2 tbsps. vegetable oil
1 tbsp. Shaoxing rice wine
1 tbsp. light soy sauce
1 tsp. Chinese five spice powder
1 tsp. cornstarch
½ tsp. light brown sugar
Kosher salt

DIRECTIONS:

1. Stir together the light soy, rice wine, five spice powder, cornstarch and brown sugar in a mixing bowl. Add the pork and mix slowly to combine. Keep aside to marinate for about 10 minutes.
2. Heat a wok over high heat until a drop of water sizzles and evaporates on contact. Add the oil and swirl to coat the base of the wok well. Season the oil with the garlic and a pinch of salt. Let the garlic sizzle in the oil for 10 seconds, swirling slowly.
3. Place pork to the wok and leave it to sear against the wok's walls for about 1 to 2 minutes, or until a golden crust develops. Gently flip and sear on the other side for another minute more. Toss and flip to stir-fry the pork for about 1 to 2 more minutes, breaking it up into crumbles and clumps until no longer pink.
4. Put the bok choy and carrot and toss and flip to combine well with the pork. Keep stir-frying for about 2 to 3 minutes, until the carrot and bok choy are soft. Transfer to a platter and serve warm with steamed rice.

Beef Empanadas

Prep Time: 30 minutes, Cook Time: 20 minutes, Serves: 6

INGREDIENTS:

9 ounces (255 g) minced beef
6 phyllo pastry sheets
6 Laughing Cow cheese wedges
2 eggs, beaten
1 onion, chopped
1½ cups parsley, finely chopped
1 pinch cinnamon
Vegetable oil
Salt and pepper to taste

DIRECTIONS:
1. In a large wok over medium heat, heat a splash of oil.
2. Cook the onion for about 3 minutes. Stir in the beef and cook it for about 5 minutes.
3. Toss in the parsley, cinnamon, a pinch of salt and pepper.
4. Stir in the beaten eggs until they are done. Remove from the heat and allow it to cool down.
5. Get a phyllo sheet. Place 2 to 3 tbsps. of the fillings on one side of it. Top it with cheese.
6. Pull the sheet sides to the middle then roll the sheet further over the filling tightly.
7. Brush the edge with beaten egg or some water. Repeat this with the remaining filling and sheets.
8. In a large deep wok over medium heat, heat 1.5 inches of oil.
9. Cook the empanadas until they turn golden brown. Drain them and put them on paper towels to drain.
10. Serve hot.

Quick Peking-Style Pork Ribs

Prep Time: 25 minutes, Cook Time: 5 minutes, Serves: 4 to 6

INGREDIENTS:
MARINADE:
2 pounds (907 g) pork ribs, cut into about 1½-inch pieces
3 tsps. cornstarch
2 tsps. Chinese rose wine
¼ tsp. five-spice powder
½ tsp. salt
Pinch ground white pepper

SAUCE:
1½ tbsps. apple cider vinegar
2 tbsps. ketchup
1 tsp. soy sauce
2 tsps. brown sugar
½ tsp. dark soy sauce
Pinch five-spice powder

STIR-FRY:
2 garlic cloves, minced
2 tbsps. peanut oil

DIRECTIONS:
1. Add the Chinese rose wine over the pork. Place the salt, pepper and five-spice powder. Combine well, then coat the pork with the cornstarch. Marinate at room temperature for about 20 minutes.
2. Prepare the sauce by mixing together the ketchup, apple cider vinegar, brown sugar, dark soy sauce, soy sauce and five-spice powder in a small bowl.
3. In a wok, heat the peanut oil over medium-high heat.
4. Place the pork ribs in the wok in a single layer. Cook without stirring for 30 seconds, turn the heat to medium, and stir-fry for 5 minutes or until the pork is cooked and golden brown.
5. Put the garlic and stir-fry for 20 seconds until fragrant.
6. Toss in the sauce, coating the ribs evenly.
7. Take the ribs and sauce to a serving plate. Serve warm.

Stir-Fried Pork Ribs with Black Bean Sauce

Prep Time: 25 minutes, Cook Time: 25 minutes, Serves: 4 to 6

INGREDIENTS:
MARINADE:
2 pounds (907 g) pork ribs, cut into 1½-inch pieces
2 tsps. cornstarch
2 tsps. Shaoxing wine
½ tsp. salt
Pinch ground white pepper
SAUCE:
2 tbsps. black bean sauce
1½ cups water
2 tsps. soy sauce
2 tsps. sugar
1 tsp. dark soy sauce
STIR-FRY:
2 garlic cloves, minced
1-inch piece ginger, peeled and minced
1 scallion, chopped
2 tbsps. peanut oil

DIRECTIONS:
1. Add the Shaoxing wine, cornstarch, salt, and pepper over the pork in a large bowl and toss to combine well. Marinate at room temperature for 20 minutes.
2. Prepare the sauce by mixing together the water, black bean sauce, sugar, soy sauce, and dark soy sauce in a small bowl. Keep aside.
3. In a wok, heat the peanut oil over medium-high heat.
4. Place the pork ribs in the wok in a single layer. Allow them to cook without stirring for about 30 seconds. Put the ginger and garlic, then gently flip the ribs with a wok spatula.
5. Cook, stirring every 10 seconds or so, for 2 minutes.
6. Add the sauce, stir often, and cover the wok.
7. Turn the heat to low and simmer for 20 minutes. Peek every few minutes to make sure the sauce is not evaporating too quickly. If it is, add more water when necessary to keep it simmering until the last minute.
8. Take the ribs to a serving plate and sprinkle with the chopped scallion. Serve hot.

Chapter 11 Pork, Beef and Lamb

Beef and Butternut Squash Stir Fry

Prep Time: 20 minutes, Cook Time: 20 minutes, Serves: 4

INGREDIENTS:

1 pound (454 g) flank beef steak, cut diagonally into 2 inch strips
½ small butternut squash, peeled, seeded, and thinly sliced
1 (8-ounce / 227-g) package dry Chinese noodles
3 cups cabbage, thinly sliced
1 cup sliced fresh mushrooms
1 tangerine, sectioned and seeded
1 large red onion, cut into 2 inch strips
¼ cup hoisin sauce
¼ cup dry sherry
2 tsps. vegetable oil
1 tsp. tangerine zest
¼ tsp. ground ginger

DIRECTIONS:

1. According to the directions on the package, cook the noodles.
2. Mix the hoisin sauce, sherry, tangerine zest and ground ginger in a small bowl.
3. In a wok over medium heat, heat the oil. Place half of the beef and brown it for about 4 minutes. Set aside and repeat this with the rest of the beef.
4. In the same wok, heat the rest of the oil. Cook the mushrooms, butternut squash and onion for about 8 minutes.
5. Stir in the cabbage and cook for about 3 minutes. Place the beef, tangerine sections, and hoisin mixture and cook for about 4 minutes. Serve your stir fry hot.

Italian Sausage Pot Pie

Prep Time: 15 minutes, Cook Time: 50 minutes, Serves: 8

INGREDIENTS:

1 pound (454 g) ground sausage
1 (15-ounce / 425-g) package pastry for a 9-inch double-crust pie
1 (14-ounce / 397-g) jar marinara sauce
10 pepperoni slices
2 cups shredded Mozzarella cheese
1 yellow onion, diced
1 green bell pepper, diced
Italian seasoning to taste
Garlic powder to taste

DIRECTIONS:

1. Preheat your oven to 350ºF (180ºC).
2. In a large wok on medium-high heat, cook the sausage for 5 to 7 minutes.
3. Drain the grease from the wok.
4. Put 1 pie crust into the bottom of a 9-inch cake pan and tightly press to fit.
5. Mix together the sausage, marinara, bell pepper and onion in a bowl.
6. Add the filling mixture in the bottom crust and top with the Mozzarella cheese.
7. Cover with the second crust and slowly crimp the edges to seal the filling.
8. Carefully, make an X in the top crust and scatter with the Italian seasoning and garlic powder.
9. Spread the pepperoni on top evenly.
10. Cook in the oven for about 35 to 45 minutes.
11. Serve warm.

Stir-Fried Ginger Lamb

Prep Time: 15 minutes, Cook Time: 15 minutes, Serves: 4

INGREDIENTS:

1 pound (454 g) boneless leg of lamb, cut into ¼-inch-thick slices
4 peeled fresh ginger slices, each about the size of a quarter
4 scallions, cut into 3-inch-long pieces, then thinly sliced lengthwise
3 garlic cloves, minced
2 whole dried red chili peppers (optional)
3 tbsps. vegetable oil, divided
2 tbsps. Shaoxing rice wine
1 tbsp. dark soy sauce
2 tsps. cornstarch
1 tsp. sesame oil
Kosher salt

DIRECTIONS:

1. Stir together the rice wine, dark soy, garlic, cornstarch and sesame oil in a large bowl. Place the lamb to the marinade and toss to coat well. Marinate for about 10 minutes.
2. Heat a wok over high heat until a drop of water sizzles and evaporates on contact. Add 2 tbsps. of vegetable oil and swirl to coat the base of the wok well. Season the oil with the ginger, chilies (if using) and a pinch of salt. Let the aromatics sizzle in the oil for 30 seconds, swirling slowly.
3. Lift half the lamb from the marinade with tongs, shaking slightly to let the excess drip off. Reserve the marinade. Sear in the wok for about 2 to 3 minutes. Gently flip to sear on the other side for another 1 to 2 minutes. Stir-fry by tossing and flipping around in the wok immediately for 1 more minute. Transfer the lamb to a clean bowl. Pour in the remaining 1 tbsp. of vegetable oil and repeat this with the remaining lamb.
4. Take all of the lamb and the reserved marinade back to the wok and toss in the scallions. Stir-fry for another 1 minute, or until the lamb is cooked through and the marinade turns into a shiny sauce.
5. Transfer the lamb to a serving platter, discard the ginger and serve warm.

Easy Quesadillas

Prep Time: 10 minutes, Cook Time: 5 minutes, Serves: 2

INGREDIENTS:

2 (8 inch) flour tortillas
½ cup leftover corned beef brisket, shredded
½ cup shredded Monterey Jack cheese
2 tbsps. diced green chilies

DIRECTIONS:

1. Place the corned beef and microwave on High for 30 to 60 seconds in a microwave safe bowl.
2. Heat a wok over medium heat.
3. In the hot wok, add 1 tortilla and top with the corned beef, Monterey Jack cheese and green chilies.
4. Cover with the other tortilla and heat for 2 to 4 minutes per side.
5. Slice in half and serve hot.

Lamb Leg with Ginger and Leeks

Prep Time: 10 minutes, Cook Time: 15 minutes, Serves: 4

INGREDIENTS:

¾ pound (340 g) boneless leg of lamb, cut into 3 chunks, then thinly sliced across the grain
2 leeks, trimmed and thinly sliced
4 garlic cloves, finely minced
2 tbsps. vegetable oil
2 tbsps. Shaoxing rice wine
1 tbsp. peeled and finely minced fresh ginger
1 tbsp. dark soy sauce
1 tbsp. light soy sauce
1 to 2 tsps. sesame oil
2 tsps. cornstarch
1 tsp. oyster sauce
1 tsp. honey
½ tsp. ground Sichuan pepper corns
Kosher salt

DIRECTIONS:

1. Season the lamb lightly with 1 to 2 pinches of salt in a mixing bowl. Toss to coat and set aside for about 10 minutes. Stir together the rice wine, light soy, dark soy, oyster sauce, honey, sesame oil, Sichuan pepper and cornstarch in a small bowl. Set aside.
2. Heat a wok over high heat until a drop of water sizzles and evaporates on contact. Add the vegetable oil and swirl to coat the base of the wok well. Season the oil with the ginger and a pinch of salt. Let the ginger sizzle in the oil for about 10 seconds, swirling slowly.
3. Add the lamb and sear for about 1 to 2 minutes, then begin to stir-fry, gently tossing and flipping for 2 minutes more, or until no longer pink. Transfer the lamb to a clean bowl and set aside.
4. Add the garlic and leeks and stir-fry for about 1 to 2 minutes, or until the leeks are bright green and tender. Transfer to the lamb bowl.
5. Add the sauce mixture and simmer for about 3 to 4 minutes, until the sauce reduces by half and becomes glossy. Take the lamb and vegetables back to the wok and toss to combine with the sauce.
6. Transfer the dish to a platter and serve warm.

Sichuan Cumin-Spiced Lamb

Prep Time: 20 minutes, Cook Time: 15 minutes, Serves: 4

INGREDIENTS:

¾ pound (340 g) boneless leg of lamb, cut into 1-inch pieces
½ yellow onion, sliced lengthwise into strips
6 to 8 whole dried Chinese chili peppers (optional)
4 garlic cloves, thinly sliced
4 peeled fresh ginger slices, each about the size of a quarter
½ bunch fresh cilantro, coarsely chopped
3 tbsps. vegetable oil, divided
2 tbsps. ground cumin
2 tbsps. cornstarch
1 tbsp. light soy sauce
1 tbsp. Shaoxing rice wine
1 tsp. Sichuan peppercorns, crushed
½ tsp. sugar
Kosher salt

DIRECTIONS:

1. Combine the lamb, light soy, rice wine and a small pinch of salt in a mixing bowl. Toss to coat well and marinate for about 15 minutes, or overnight in the refrigerator.
2. Stir together the cumin, Sichuan peppercorns and sugar in another bowl. Keep aside.
3. Heat a wok over high heat until a drop of water sizzles and evaporates on contact. Add 2 tbsps. of oil and swirl to coat the base of the wok well. Season the oil with the ginger and a pinch of salt. Let the ginger sizzle in the oil for 30 seconds, swirling slowly.
4. Toss the lamb pieces with the cornstarch and add them to the hot wok. Sear the lamb for about 2 to 3 minutes per side, and then stir-fry for 1 or 2 minutes more, gently tossing and flipping around the wok. Transfer the lamb to a clean bowl and keep aside.
5. Pour in the remaining 1 tbsp. of oil and swirl to coat the wok well. Toss in the onion and chili peppers (if using) and stir-fry for about 3 to 4 minutes, or until the onion begins to turn shiny but not limp. Season lightly with a small pinch of salt. Stir in the garlic and spice mixture and continue to stir-fry for 1 minute.
6. Take the lamb back to the wok and toss to combine for about 1 to 2 minutes more. Transfer the lamb to a platter. Remove and discard the ginger and garnish with the cilantro. Serve warm.

Lamb with Pear and Prunes

Prep Time: 10 minutes, Cook Time: 1 hour, Serves: 8

INGREDIENTS:

2½ pounds (1.1 kg) lamb, cubed
1 pear, peeled and cubed
16 prunes, soaked and drained
3 cups water
¼ cup orange juice
¼ cup sugar
3 tbsps. butter
2 tbsps. almonds
2 tbsps. raisins
½ tsp. ground cinnamon
1 tsp. orange blossom water

DIRECTIONS:

1. In a large wok over medium heat, heat the butter until it melts.
2. Cook the lamb for about 6 minutes. Toss in the cinnamon with sugar and water.
3. Cook for about 42 minutes while stirring constantly with the lid on.
4. Once the time is up, stir in the prunes, almonds, raisins, pear and orange blossom water.
5. Cook for another 16 minutes until the sauce turns thick.
6. Stir in the orange juice and cook for about 5 minutes.
7. Adjust the seasoning of your stew then serve warm.

Pork Ribs with Black Bean Sauce

Prep Time: 15 minutes, Cook Time: 20 minutes, Serves: 4

INGREDIENTS:

1 pound (454 g) pork spareribs, cut crosswise into 1½-inch-wide strips
½-inch fresh ginger piece, peeled and finely minced
2 garlic cloves, finely minced
2 scallions, thinly sliced
2 tbsps. store-bought black bean sauce
1 tbsp. Shaoxing rice wine
1 tbsp. vegetable oil
2 tsps. cornstarch
1 tsp. sesame oil
¼ tsp. ground white pepper

DIRECTIONS:

1. Slice between the ribs to separate them into bite-size riblets. Combine the ribs and white pepper in a shallow, heatproof bowl. Place the black bean sauce, rice wine, vegetable oil, cornstarch, garlic and ginger and toss to combine well, making sure the riblets are all coated. Marinate for about 10 minutes.
2. Rinse a bamboo steamer basket and its lid with cold water and put it in the wok. Add 2 inches of water, or until it reaches above the bottom rim of the steamer by about ¼ to ½ inch, but not so much that it touches the bottom of the basket. Arrange the bowl with the ribs in the steamer basket and cover.
3. Increase the heat to high to boil the water, then turn the heat to medium-high. Steam over medium-high heat for about 20 to 22 minutes, or until the riblets are no longer pink. You should replenish the water, so keep checking to make sure it doesn't boil dry in the wok.
4. Take the bowl carefully from the steamer basket. Drizzle the ribs with the sesame oil and sprinkle with the scallions. Serve hot.

Beef Tenderloin with Shiitake Mushrooms

Prep Time: 25 minutes, Cook Time: 5 minutes, Serves: 4 to 6

INGREDIENTS:

5 cups boiling water
2 cups whole dried shiitake mushrooms
MARINADE:
1 pound (454 g) beef tenderloin or sirloin, cut into thin strips
2 tsps. cornstarch
2 tsps. soy sauce
Pinch freshly ground black pepper
SAUCE:
½ tsp. sesame oil
2 tbsps. oyster sauce
1 tbsp. soy sauce
2 tsps. brown sugar
STIR-FRY:
1 scallion, chopped
2 tbsps. peanut oil

DIRECTIONS:

1. Soak the dried shiitake mushrooms in boiling water for 20 minutes.
2. At the same time, add the soy sauce, cornstarch and pepper over the beef in a large bowl, and toss to combine well. Marinate at room temperature for 20 minutes.
3. Make the sauce by mixing together the oyster sauce, soy sauce, brown sugar and sesame oil in a small bowl. Keep aside.
4. Drain and pour out the water from the mushrooms, cut off and discard the mushroom stems, and slowly squeeze the caps to remove excess water.
5. Slice the mushrooms into thin slices.
6. In a wok, heat the peanut oil over medium-high heat.
7. Add the beef and stir-fry for 30 seconds, then remove it from the wok.
8. Place the sliced mushrooms, along with a little more peanut oil if needed. Stir-fry for another 2 minutes, then stir in the sauce.
9. Take the beef back to the wok, toss to combine all the ingredients, and transfer the dish to a serving plate.
10. Sprinkle with the chopped scallion and serve hot.

Mongolian Beef Steak

Prep Time: 25 minutes, Cook Time: 5 minutes, Serves: 4

INGREDIENTS:
MARINADE:
1 pound (454 g) flank steak or sirloin steak, thinly sliced
2 tsps. cornstarch
½ tsp. salt
Pinch freshly ground black pepper
SAUCE:
1 tbsp. water
1 tbsp. soy sauce
1 tsp. rice vinegar
1 tsp. brown sugar
STIR-FRY:
2 tbsps. peanut oil
2 garlic cloves, minced
1 scallion, cut into 1-inch pieces
1-inch piece ginger, peeled and julienned

DIRECTIONS:
1. Sprinkle the cornstarch, salt and pepper over the beef in a large bowl and toss to combine well. Marinate at room temperature for about 20 minutes.
2. Prepare the sauce by mixing together the soy sauce, brown sugar, water and rice vinegar in a small bowl.
3. In a wok, heat the peanut oil over medium-high heat.
4. Place the beef and fry just until the surfaces turn brown.
5. Add the garlic and ginger and stir-fry until fragrant, about 2 or 3 seconds.
6. Add the sauce and stir to coat the beef evenly.
7. Remove from the heat and add the scallion. Give it one last stir to very lightly heat up the scallions but not to cook them.
8. Transfer the beef to a serving plate. Serve warm.

Beef with Honey and Oyster Sauce

Prep Time: 15 minutes, Cook Time: 5 minutes, Serves: 4 to 6

INGREDIENTS:
MARINADE:
1 pound (454 g) beef tenderloin or steak, cut into thin slices
3 tsps. cornstarch
½ tsp. salt
¼ tsp. black pepper
SAUCE:
3 tbsps. honey
2 tsps. oyster sauce
2½ tbsps. low-sodium soy sauce
1 tsp. freshly ground black pepper
2 tbsps. water
STIR-FRY:
½ onion, thinly sliced
2 garlic cloves, minced
2 tbsps. peanut oil

DIRECTIONS:
1. Sprinkle the cornstarch, salt and pepper over the beef in a large bowl and toss to combine well. Marinate at room temperature for about 15 minutes.
2. Prepare the sauce by mixing together the honey, oyster sauce, soy sauce, water and pepper in a small bowl.
3. In a wok, heat the peanut oil over medium-high heat.
4. Place the beef and stir-fry until just browned, remove from the wok, and keep aside.
5. Toss the onion and garlic into the wok and stir-fry until the onion looks slightly translucent.
6. Take the beef back to the wok and add the sauce, stirring to coat the beef evenly.
7. Remove from the heat and transfer the beef to a serving plate. Serve warm.

Beef Steak and Bell Peppers Stir-Fry

Prep Time: 25 minutes, Cook Time: 5 minutes, Serves: 4 to 6

INGREDIENTS:
MARINADE:
1 pound (454 g) flank steak, thinly sliced
2 tsps. cornstarch
½ tsp. salt
½ tsp. ground black pepper
SAUCE:
1 tbsp. soy sauce
1 tsp. black bean sauce
½ tsp. sesame oil
½ tsp. sugar
½ tsp. dark soy sauce
STIR-FRY:
1 red bell pepper, cut into thin strips
1 green bell pepper, cut into thin strips
1 onion, cut into rings
1 fresh red or green chile, cut into strips (optional)
2 cloves garlic, minced
2 tbsps. peanut oil

DIRECTIONS:
1. Sprinkle the cornstarch, salt, and pepper over the beef in a large bowl and toss to combine well. Marinate at room temperature for 20 minutes.
2. Prepare the sauce by mixing together the black bean sauce, soy sauce, dark soy sauce, sugar and sesame oil in a small bowl. Keep aside.
3. In a wok, heat the peanut oil over high heat.
4. Place the beef in the wok in a single layer. Cook without stirring for 20 seconds, gently flip the beef, and continue to stir-fry until completely cooked, for 1 minute.
5. Take the beef from the wok.
6. Pour a little more oil to the wok if needed, then put the garlic, red and green bell peppers, onion and chile (if using). Avoid stirring too much, just toss lightly so the high heat can blister the peppers.
7. Take the beef back to the wok and add the sauce. Stir to combine all the ingredients and take the dish to a serving plate. Serve warm.

Honey Pork

Prep Time: 25 minutes, Cook Time: 5 minutes, Serves: 4 to 6

INGREDIENTS:
MARINADE:
1 pound (454 g) pork tenderloin or shoulder, cut into thin strips
2 tsps. cornstarch
2 tsps. Shaoxing wine
½ tsp. Chinese five-spice powder
½ tsp. salt
Pinch ground white pepper

SAUCE:
2 tsps. honey
1 tbsp. soy sauce
½ tsp. Chinese five-spice powder
½ tsp. brown sugar
½ tsp. dark soy sauce

STIR-FRY:
2 garlic cloves, minced
2 tbsps. peanut oil

DIRECTIONS:
1. Add the Shaoxing wine, cornstarch, five-spice powder, salt and pepper over the pork in a large bowl and toss to combine well. Marinate at room temperature for about 20 minutes.
2. Prepare the sauce by combining the soy sauce, honey, brown sugar, dark soy sauce, and five-spice powder in a small bowl.
3. In a wok, heat the peanut oil over medium-high heat.
4. Place the pork and stir-fry until slightly golden brown.
5. Add the garlic and stir-fry for 20 seconds.
6. Stir in the sauce, tossing well to coat the pork, and take the pork to a serving dish. Serve hot.

Steamed Egg with Ground Pork

Prep Time: 15 minutes, Cook Time: 15 minutes, Serves: 4 to 6

INGREDIENTS:
½ pound (227 g) ground pork
2 tsps. finely diced Chinese preserved radish (optional)
2 tsps. soy sauce
1 tsp. cornstarch
½ tsp. salt
Pinch freshly ground black pepper
3 eggs
½ cup water
1 tsp. Shaoxing wine

DIRECTIONS:
1. In a medium bowl, combine the ground pork, preserved radish (if using), soy sauce, cornstarch, salt, and pepper, mixing it well. Marinate at room temperature for about 15 minutes.
2. Set up a steaming rack in a wok, fill it with water halfway up to the rack, and set the heat to medium.
3. In a separate bowl, whisk the eggs with the water and Shaoxing wine. Set it aside.
4. Transfer the ground pork mixture to a shallow heatproof dish. Spread the ground pork in a single layer to cover the dish.
5. Pour the egg mixture evenly over the ground pork.
6. Cover the dish with aluminum foil. This will prevent water from dripping onto the custard.
7. When the water in the wok starts to boil, place the dish on the steaming rack.
8. Steam for about 15 minutes or until the custard is set, then serve.

Sichuan Twice-Cooked Pork with Leek

Prep Time: 25 minutes, Cook Time: 5 minutes, Serves: 4

INGREDIENTS:
1 pound (454 g) pork shoulder
Water for boiling pork shoulder
SAUCE:
1 tbsp. black bean paste
1 tbsp. soy sauce
1 tsp. chili bean paste
½ tsp. sugar
Pinch salt
STIR-FRY:
1 leek, cut into 1-inch pieces
1 green bell pepper, cut into bite-size pieces
2 garlic cloves, minced
1 tbsp. peanut oil

DIRECTIONS:
1. Cover the pork shoulder with enough water in a medium pot. Bring the water to a boil over high heat and place the pork into the pot.
2. Turn the heat to medium, cover and simmer for about 20 minutes.
3. Take the pork from the water and allow it to cool. Keep it in the refrigerator until you are ready to cook the dish.
4. Prepare the sauce by mixing together the black bean paste, soy sauce, chili bean paste, sugar and salt in a small bowl.
5. Once the meat has cooled and you are ready to prepare the dish, cut it into the thinnest pieces possible with a very sharp knife.
6. In a wok, heat the peanut oil over medium-high heat.
7. Place the pork and stir-fry the slices until they turn slightly brown around the edges. Take the pork from the wok and keep aside.
8. Pour more oil to the wok if needed, add the garlic and stir-fry for 20 seconds, until fragrant.
9. Add the leek and bell pepper, stir-fry for 1 minute, and take the pork back to the wok.
10. Put the black bean sauce, stir well, and transfer the dish to a serving plate. Serve warm.

Beef Ramen with Pepperoni Stir-Fry

Prep Time: 10 minutes, Cook Time: 15 minutes, Serves: 6

INGREDIENTS:
1 pound (454 g) ground beef, or to taste
16 slices pepperoni, or to taste
1 (14½-ounce / 411-g) can diced tomatoes
2 (3-ounce / 85-g) packages beef-flavored ramen noodles
1 cup shredded Mozzarella cheese
1 green bell peppers, cut into strips
1 cup water

DIRECTIONS:
1. In a large wok over high heat, cook the beef and pepperoni slices for 7 minutes before placing tomatoes, content of seasoning packet content from ramen noodles and water into wok containing beef.
2. After breaking ramen noodles into half, put this to the beef mixture along with green bell pepper and cook for 5 minutes or until that noodles are soft.
3. Remove from the heat before adding Mozzarella cheese. Allow it to melt down before serving.

Sichuan Beef with Carrot

Prep Time: 15 minutes, Cook Time: 5 minutes, Serves: 4

INGREDIENTS:
MARINADE:
1 pound (454 g) beef tenderloin or sirloin, cut into ¼-inch strips (like French fries)
1 tsp. sesame oil
2 tsps. cornstarch
1 tsp. soy sauce
SAUCE:
1 tbsp. soy sauce
1 tsp. sesame oil
1 tsp. chili oil
1 tsp. brown sugar
½ tbsp. oyster sauce
¼ tsp. dark soy sauce
STIR-FRY:
2 tbsps. peanut oil
½ carrot, julienned
5 or 6 dried red chiles
2 garlic cloves, minced
1 scallion, chopped

DIRECTIONS:
1. Add the cornstarch, sesame oil, and soy sauce over the beef in a large bowl and toss to combine well. Marinate at room temperature for about 15 minutes.
2. Prepare the sauce by mixing together the soy sauce, brown sugar, sesame oil, chili oil, oyster sauce and dark soy sauce in a small bowl. Keep aside.
3. In a wok, heat the peanut oil over medium-high heat.
4. Place the beef and stir-fry for 30 seconds.
5. Add the garlic and stir-fry until the beef is almost cooked.
6. Pour in the sauce and dried red chiles, tossing to combine all the ingredients evenly.
7. Remove from the heat, put the carrot and give the dish one last stir.
8. Transfer the beef to a serving plate and sprinkle with the chopped scallion. Serve warm.

Twice-Cooked Pork Belly with Black Bean Sauce

Prep Time: 10 minutes, Cook Time: 45 minutes, Serves: 4

INGREDIENTS:
1 pound (454 g) boneless pork belly
⅓ cup store-bought black bean sauce
1 leek, halved lengthwise and cut on the diagonal into ½-inch slices
½ red bell pepper, sliced
4 peeled fresh ginger slices, each about the size of a quarter
2 tbsps. vegetable oil, divided
1 tbsp. Shaoxing rice wine
1 tsp. dark soy sauce
½ tsp. sugar
Kosher salt

DIRECTIONS:
1. In a large saucepan, add the pork and cover with water. Bring the pan to a boil over high heat and then reduce to a simmer. Simmer uncovered for about 30 minutes, or until the pork is soft and cooked through. Transfer the pork to a bowl (discard the cooking liquid) with a slotted spoon and allow to cool. Refrigerate for several hours or overnight. When the pork is cool, thinly slice into ¼-inch-thick slices and keep aside. Letting the pork cool completely before slicing will make it easier to thinly slice.
2. Stir together the black bean sauce, rice wine, dark soy and sugar in a glass measuring cup, and set aside.
3. Heat a wok over high heat until a drop of water sizzles and evaporates on contact. Add 1 tbsp. of oil and swirl to coat the base of the wok well. Season the oil with the ginger and a pinch of salt. Let the ginger sizzle in the oil for 30 seconds, swirling slowly.
4. Transfer half the pork to the wok, working in batches. Let the pieces sear in the wok for about 2 to 3 minutes. Flip to sear on the other side for about 1 to 2 minutes more, until the pork begins to curl. Take the pork to a clean bowl. Repeat this with the remaining pork.
5. Pour in the remaining 1 tbsp. of oil. Add the leek and red pepper and stir-fry for about 1 minute, until the leek is tender. Swirl in the sauce and stir-fry until aromatic. Take the pork back to the pan and continue stir-frying for 2 to 3 more minutes, until everything is just cooked through. Remove and discard the ginger slices and transfer to a serving platter. Serve warm.

Andouille and Basmati Rice

Prep Time: 5 minutes, Cook Time: 50 minutes, Serves: 1

INGREDIENTS:

2 cups water
1 cup basmati rice, rinsed in cold water
½ pound (227 g) andouille sausages, sliced

DIRECTIONS:

1. In a 10-inch wok over medium heat, place the sausage slices and ½ cup of the water and cook, covered for 15 minutes.
2. Open the lid and cook the sausage until all the liquid is absorbed completely.
3. Put the rice and stir fry until browned.
4. Toss in the remaining water and bring to a boil.
5. Turn the heat to low and simmer, covered for 10 to 12 minutes.
6. Turn off the heat and set aide, covered for 30 minutes.
7. Fluff the rice with a fork and serve warm.

Sesame Carrots and Steak Stir Fry

Prep Time: 20 minutes, Cook Time: 15 minutes, Serves: 6

INGREDIENTS:

1½ pounds (680 g) beef top round steak, cut into thin slices
2 carrots, cut into matchstick-size pieces
2 eggs, beaten
1 green onion, chopped
5 cloves garlic, chopped
1 cup oil for frying, or as needed
1 cup cornstarch
½ cup water
½ cup white sugar
¼ cup soy sauce
5 tbsps. minced fresh ginger root
2 tbsps. white vinegar
1 tbsp. sesame oil
1 tbsp. sesame seeds, or as needed
¼ tsp. red pepper flakes

DIRECTIONS:

1. Mix the water with cornstarch in a small bowl. Place the beef slices and toss them to coat well.
2. In a wok over medium heat, heat 2 to 3 inches of oil. Deep fry the beef slices in batches for about 5 minutes per batch. Drain them and set aside.
3. In a wok over medium heat, heat the sesame oil. Put the carrots, ginger, green onion and garlic. Cook for about 6 minutes.
4. Add the white vinegar, soy sauce, sugar and red pepper flakes. Cook them until they start boiling. Place the cooked beef slices with sesame seeds.
5. Serve your stir fry hot.

Orange Sesame Beef

Prep Time: 15 minutes, Cook Time: 10 minutes, Serves: 4

INGREDIENTS:

1 pound (454 g) hanger, skirt, or flat iron steak, cut into ¼-inch-thick strips
½ cup freshly squeezed orange juice
1 small yellow onion, thinly sliced
4 peeled fresh ginger slices, each about the size of a quarter
3 garlic cloves, minced
3 tbsps. vegetable oil, divided
2 tbsps. sesame oil, divided
1 tbsp. light soy sauce
½ tbsp. white sesame seeds, for garnish
2 tsps. cornstarch, divided
1 tsp. sriracha (optional)
1 tsp. light brown sugar
½ tsp. rice vinegar
Kosher salt
Freshly ground black pepper

DIRECTIONS:

1. Stir together the light soy, 1 tbsp. of sesame oil, and 1 tsp. of cornstarch in a large bowl, until the cornstarch dissolves. Place the beef and toss to coat in the marinade. Keep aside to marinate for about 10 minutes while you prep the sauce.
2. Stir together the remaining 1 tbsp. of sesame oil, orange juice, rice vinegar, sriracha (if using), brown sugar, remaining 1 tsp. of cornstarch, a pinch each of salt and pepper in a glass measuring cup. Stir until the cornstarch is dissolved entirely and keep aside.
3. Heat a wok over high heat until a drop of water sizzles and evaporates on contact. Add 2 tbsps. of vegetable oil and swirl to coat the base of the wok well. Season the oil with the ginger and a pinch of salt. Let the ginger sizzle in the oil for 30 seconds, swirling slowly.
4. Transfer the beef to the wok and discard the marinade with tongs. Let the pieces sear in the wok for about 2 to 3 minutes. Flip to sear on the other side for extra 1 to 2 minutes. Stir-fry by tossing and flipping around in the wok immediately for 1 more minute. Transfer to a clean bowl.
5. Pour in the remaining 1 tbsp. of vegetable oil and toss in the onion. Quickly stir-fry, using a wok spatula to toss and flip the onion for 2 to 3 minutes, until the onion turns translucent but is still firm in texture. Place the garlic and stir-fry for another 30 seconds.
6. Swirl in the sauce and continue to cook until the sauce starts to thicken.Take the beef back to the wok, tossing and flipping so the beef and onion are evenly coated with sauce. Season with salt and pepper to taste.
7. Take the beef to a platter, discard the ginger, scatter with the sesame seeds. Serve hot.

Chapter 11 Pork, Beef and Lamb

Corned Beef

Prep Time: 15 minutes, Cook Time: 15 minutes, Serves: 4

INGREDIENTS:

- 1 (12-ounce / 340-g) can corned beef
- ¼ onion, chopped
- ¼ cup water
- 2 tsps. tomato paste
- 1 tsp. vegetable oil
- ¼ tsp. crushed red pepper flakes
- ¼ tsp. dried thyme
- ¼ green bell pepper, chopped
- Salt and pepper to taste

DIRECTIONS:

1. In a large wok over medium heat, heat the oil and sauté the green pepper, onion, red pepper flakes and dried thyme for 7 minutes.
2. Turn the heat to low and toss in the tomato paste, salt and pepper.
3. Simmer for 3 minutes.
4. Stir in the corned beef and water and simmer until all the liquid is absorbed. Serve warm.

Beef with Cranberry Sauce

Prep Time: 25 minutes, Cook Time: 20 minutes, Serves: 6

INGREDIENTS:

- 2 pounds (907 g) cubed beef stew meat
- 1 (14-ounce / 397-g) can jellied cranberry sauce
- ¾ cup broccoli florets
- ¾ cup sliced carrot
- ¾ cup sugar snap peas
- ¾ cup sliced onion
- 3 tbsps. olive oil
- 2 tbsps. lemon juice
- 1 tbsp. minced garlic
- 1 tsp. ground ginger

DIRECTIONS:

1. Combine the lemon juice with cranberry sauce in a small mixing bowl.
2. In a wok over medium heat, heat a splash of oil. Place the carrot, broccoli, snap peas and onion. Cook them for about 6 minutes. Set aside.
3. In the same wok, heat the olive oil. Cook the garlic for about 1 minute. Add the beef and cook for about 6 minutes.
4. Put the cooked veggies with cranberry sauce mix and ginger. Cook for about 6 minutes. Serve your stir fry hot.

Sweet and Sour Beef Stir Fry

Prep Time: 25 minutes, Cook Time: 15 minutes, Serves: 4

INGREDIENTS:

- 1 pound (454 g) round steak, thinly sliced
- 12 mushrooms, sliced
- 4 cups cooked rice
- 1 onion, chopped
- ¼ cup sweet and sour sauce
- 1 red bell pepper, chopped
- 1 (1 inch) piece fresh ginger root, peeled and thinly sliced
- 1 tbsp. soy sauce
- 1 tsp. butter

DIRECTIONS:

1. Stir the steak, ginger, and soy sauce in a large mixing bowl. Cover the bowl and put it in the fridge for about 35 minutes.
2. In the wok over medium heat, add the steak mix and cover the lid. Cook for about 6 minutes. Drain the beef and set aside.
3. In the same wok, heat the butter until it melts. Place the onion, bell pepper, mushrooms and sweet and sour sauce. Cover the lid and cook for about 4 minutes.
4. Turn the beef back into the wok. Cook for about 3 minutes. Serve your stir fry hot with cooked rice.

Appetizer Bok Choy, page 78

Hoisin Sesame Tofu, page 80

Five-Spice Pork Meatballs, page 80

Shrimp with Roasted Peanuts, page 76

74   Chapter 12 Snacks and Desserts

Chapter 12 Snacks and Desserts

Shrimp and Water Chestnuts Dumplings

Prep Time: 45 minutes, Cook Time: 5 minutes, Makes: 15 to 20 dumplings

INGREDIENTS:
FILLING:
1 pound (454 g) peeled and deveined shrimp, roughly chopped
¼ cup diced water chestnuts
2 tbsps. cornstarch
2 tbsps. finely chopped fresh cilantro (optional)
1½ tbsps. sesame oil
2 tsps. soy sauce
WRAPPERS:
1¼ cups wheat starch
1¼ cups boiling water
2 tbsps. tapioca flour
1 tsp. peanut oil

DIRECTIONS:
MAKE THE FILLING:
1. Combine the shrimp, water chestnuts, sesame oil, soy sauce and cornstarch in a large bowl. Add the cilantro (if using) and mix well.
2. Marinate the mixture for at least 30 minutes in the refrigerator.

MAKE THE WRAPPERS:
3. Combine the wheat starch and tapioca flour in a large bowl.
4. Gently pour the boiling water into the flour mixture while stirring, until it starts to form a ball of dough.
5. Cover the bowl with a damp towel and let the dough cool down slightly before handling.
6. Use a bit of peanut oil to cover your palms, a small rolling pin and a cutting board for preventing the dough from sticking.
7. Knead the dough for about 2 to 3 minutes.
8. Take about a tsp. of dough and slowly roll it into a ball.
9. Roll the dough out into a small pancake, about 3 inches in diameter.

MAKE THE DUMPLINGS:
10. Place a bamboo steamer in a wok. Line the steamer with parchment paper liners.
11. Put about 1 tsp. of shrimp filling in the middle of a wrapper.
12. Make pleats on one side of the wrapper, then gently fold the other side of the wrapper toward the pleated side to seal the dumpling.
13. Repeat this with the remaining filling and wrappers.
14. Arrange the dumplings in the bamboo steamer and steam for 5 minutes or until cooked through. Serve warm.

Pork and Mushroom Lettuce Wraps

Prep Time: 25 minutes, Cook Time: 5 minutes, Serves: 4 to 6

INGREDIENTS:
1 head lettuce
MARINADE:
1 pound (454 g) pork tenderloin, cut into thin strips (like French fries)
2 tsps. cornstarch
2 tsps. Shaoxing wine
2 tsps. soy sauce
½ tsp. salt
Pinch ground white pepper
SAUCE:
2 tbsps. hoisin sauce
1 tbsp. oyster sauce
1 tbsp. rice vinegar
1 tsp. soy sauce
1 tsp. sugar
½ tsp. sesame oil
STIR-FRY:
2 tbsps. peanut oil
4 cups shredded cabbage
4 or 5 large shiitake mushrooms, thinly sliced
½ carrot, julienned
½ cup chopped fresh cilantro
2 garlic cloves, minced
1 scallion, chopped
2-inch piece ginger, peeled and julienned

DIRECTIONS:
1. Separate and rinse the lettuce leaves. Chill the leaves in the refrigerator until ready to serve.
2. Add the soy sauce, Shaoxing wine, cornstarch, salt, and pepper over the pork in a large bowl and toss to combine well and coat the meat. Marinate at room temperature for about 20 minutes.
3. At the same time, make the sauce by mixing together the hoisin sauce, rice vinegar, oyster sauce, sugar, soy sauce and sesame oil in a small bowl. Keep it aside.
4. In a wok, heat the peanut oil over medium-high heat.
5. Add the garlic and ginger and stir-fry until fragrant, or for 20 seconds.
6. Place the pork and stir-fry for 30 seconds.
7. Toss in the sliced shiitake mushrooms.
8. When the pork and mushrooms are cooked completely, stir in the sauce and mix well.
9. Toss in the carrot and shredded cabbage, stir, and remove from the heat.
10. Transfer the dish to a serving plate and garnish with the chopped scallion and cilantro. Serve with the chilled lettuce.

Japanese Cumin Chicken Stir Fry

Prep Time: 20 minutes, Cook Time: 15 minutes, Serves: 4

INGREDIENTS:
- 1 (3-pound / 1.4-kg) whole chicken, cut into pieces
- ⅔ cup soy sauce
- ¼ cup mirin
- 1 clove garlic, crushed
- 3 tbsps. white sugar
- 2 tbsps. cooking oil
- 1 tbsp. grated fresh ginger root
- 1 tbsp. sake

DIRECTIONS:
1. Clean the chicken and pat it dry with a paper towel.
2. Mix the ginger, garlic, sugar, soy sauce, sake and mirin in a glass oven pan. Add the chicken pieces and stir them to coat evenly.
3. Cover the dish with a plastic wrap and put it in the fridge for about 2 hours to 8 hours.
4. In a large wok over medium heat, heat the oil. Drain the chicken pieces from the marinade and fry them until they turn golden brown.
5. Drain the chicken pieces and set them aside. Take the grease from the pan. Pour the marinade from the chicken into the wok with the browned chicken pieces.
6. Turn the heat to low and cover the lid. Cook the marinade for about 9 minutes to make the sauce. Open the lid and keep cooking them until the chicken is done fully and the sauce is thick.
7. Serve your saucy chicken hot.

Shrimp with Roasted Peanuts

Prep Time: 5 minutes, Cook Time: 10 minutes, Serves: 4 to 6

INGREDIENTS:
SAUCE:
- 2 tsps. brown sugar
- 2 tbsps. rice vinegar
- 2 tbsps. soy sauce
- 1 tsp. sesame oil
- 1 tsp. dark soy sauce
- 1 tsp. cornstarch

STIR-FRY:
- 1 pound (454 g) shrimp, peeled and deveined
- ¼ cup unsalted roasted peanuts
- 8 to 10 dried red chiles
- 1 small green bell pepper (or ½ a large one), cut into bite-size pieces
- 2 tbsps. peanut oil
- 2-inch piece ginger, peeled and julienned
- 2 garlic cloves, minced
- 1 or 2 scallions, cut into 1-inch pieces

DIRECTIONS:
1. Prepare the sauce by combining the rice vinegar, soy sauce, brown sugar, dark soy sauce, sesame oil and cornstarch in a small bowl. Keep aside.
2. In a wok, heat the peanut oil over medium heat.
3. Add the bell pepper and chiles and stir-fry slowly, letting the skin of the bell pepper blister.
4. Add the garlic and ginger and stir-fry for 20 seconds until aromatic.
5. Place the shrimp, spreading them in a single layer. Cook the bottom side of the shrimp, then gently flip and stir-fry them for 1 minute or until completely cooked.
6. Put the roasted peanuts and stir in the sauce.
7. When the sauce thickens, remove from the heat and toss in the scallions. Transfer the dish to a serving plate and serve warm.

Egg Foo Yong with Peas

Prep Time: 15 minutes, Cook Time: 15 minutes, Serves: 4

INGREDIENTS:
- 5 large eggs, at room temperature
- ½ cup thinly sliced shiitake mushroom caps
- ½ cup frozen peas, thawed
- 2 scallions, chopped
- Cooked rice, for serving
- ½ cup low-sodium chicken broth
- 3 tbsps. vegetable oil
- 2 tbsps. light soy sauce
- 1½ tbsps. oyster sauce
- 1 tbsp. Shaoxing rice wine
- 1 tbsp. cornstarch
- 2 tsps. sesame oil
- ½ tsp. sugar
- Kosher salt
- Ground white pepper

DIRECTIONS:
1. Whisk the eggs with a pinch each of salt and white pepper. Stir in the mushrooms, peas, scallions and sesame oil in a large bowl. Keep aside.
2. In a small saucepan over medium heat, make the sauce by simmering the chicken broth, oyster sauce, rice wine and sugar. In a small glass measuring cup, slowly whisk the light soy and cornstarch until the cornstarch is entirely dissolved. Pour the cornstarch mixture into the sauce while whisking frequently and cook for about 3 to 4 minutes, until the sauce turns thick enough to coat the back of the spoon. Cover and keep aside.
3. Heat a wok over high heat until a drop of water sizzles and evaporates on contact. Add the vegetable oil and swirl to coat the base of the wok well. Add the egg mixture and cook, gently swirling and shaking the wok until the bottom side is golden. Slide the omelet out of the pan onto a plate and invert over the wok or use a spatula to turn over, then cook the other side until golden. Slide the omelet out onto a serving platter and serve over cooked rice with the sauce.

Vanilla Banana Bites

Prep Time: 10 minutes, Cook Time: 8 minutes, Serves: 2

INGREDIENTS:
1 cup vegetable oil
1 banana, peeled and cut into pieces
6 spring roll wrappers, halved
1 tbsp. powdered sugar
1 tsp. sugar
¼ tsp. vanilla

DIRECTIONS:
1. Add the banana pieces, vanilla extract and sugar in a bowl and mix well.
2. Put 1 banana piece over each spring roll wrapper half.
3. Use the wet fingers to moisten the edges and roll the wrapper around banana piece.
4. In a deep wok over high heat, add the oil and cook until heated through.
5. Place the banana wraps in batches and fry until golden from both sides.
6. Use a slotted spoon to transfer the banana wraps onto a paper towel-lined plate to drain.
7. Sprinkle with powdered sugar and enjoy.

Easy Tomato Egg Stir-Fry

Prep Time: 5 minutes, Cook Time: 10 minutes, Serves: 4

INGREDIENTS:
1 pound (454 g) grape or cherry tomatoes
4 large eggs, at room temperature
2 peeled fresh ginger slices, each about the size of a quarter
Cooked rice or noodles, for serving
3 tbsps. vegetable oil, divided
1 tsp. Shaoxing rice wine
1 tsp. sugar
½ tsp. sesame oil
½ tsp. kosher salt
Freshly ground black pepper

DIRECTIONS:
1. Whisk the eggs in a large bowl. Place the rice wine, sesame oil, salt and a pinch of pepper and continue whisking until just combined.
2. Heat a wok over high heat until a drop of water sizzles and evaporates on contact. Add 2 tbsps. of vegetable oil and swirl to coat the base of the wok well. Gently swirl the egg mixture into the hot wok. Swirl and shake the eggs to cook. Take the eggs to a serving plate when just cooked but not dry. Carefully tent with foil to keep warm.
3. Pour the remaining 1 tbsp. of vegetable oil to the wok. Season the oil with the ginger and a pinch of salt. Let the ginger sizzle in the oil for 30 seconds, swirling slowly.
4. Toss in the tomatoes and sugar, stirring to coat with the oil. Cover and cook for 5 minutes, stirring frequently, until the tomatoes are tender and have released their juices. Remove and discard the ginger slices and season the tomatoes with salt and pepper to taste.
5. Scoop the tomatoes over the eggs, and serve hot over cooked rice or noodles.

Crab Egg Foo Young Patties

Prep Time: 10 minutes, Cook Time: 20 minutes, Serves: 4 to 6

INGREDIENTS:
SAUCE:
1 tbsp. oyster sauce
1 cup chicken stock
2 tsps. cornstarch
2 tsps. soy sauce
½ tsp. sesame oil
MARINADE:
1 tsp. soy sauce
4 eggs
½ tsp. salt
Pinch ground white pepper
EGG FOO YOUNG:
1 cup cooked crab meat
2 cups fresh bean sprouts
½ small yellow onion, diced
½ cup chopped scallion
4 tbsps. peanut oil, divided
1 tbsp. water

DIRECTIONS:
1. Prepare the sauce by combining the chicken stock, oyster sauce, soy sauce, cornstarch and sesame oil in a small bowl. Keep aside.
2. Season the eggs with the soy sauce, salt and pepper in a separate bowl. Beat lightly until well combined.
3. In a wok, heat 1 tbsp. of peanut oil over medium heat.
4. Place the onion and stir-fry until translucent.
5. Pour the fresh bean sprouts and water to the wok, and stir-fry for 20 seconds.
6. When all the water has evaporated and the bean sprouts have softened a little, place the crab meat and scallions. Remove from the heat and transfer the crab mixture to a large bowl.
7. Add the eggs over the crab mixture and stir to combine well.
8. In the wok over medium-high heat, heat the remaining 3 tbsps. of peanut oil.
9. Add about ⅓ cup of the egg-crab mixture into the wok. Cook until golden brown, or for 2 minutes on each side. Keep aside. Repeat this with the remaining mixture, ⅓ cup at a time.
10. Stir the sauce well and pour it into the wok. Simmer until the sauce thickens, then scoop the sauce over the egg foo young patties. Serve warm.

Appetizer Bok Choy

Prep Time: 10 minutes, Cook Time: 25 minutes, Serves: 2

INGREDIENTS:
1 pound (454 g) baby bok choy, trimmed and sliced in half lengthwise
2 cups chicken stock
1 cup white wine
3 tbsps. butter
1 clove garlic, smashed
1 bay leaf

DIRECTIONS:
1. In a large wok over medium heat, melt the butter and cook the garlic and bay leaf for 5 minutes.
2. Toss in the chicken stock and white wine, and bring to a full boil.
3. Cook for 15 minutes, stirring constantly.
4. Remove and discard the bay leaf.
5. Put the bok choy halves, cut sides down into the sauce and reduce heat.
6. Simmer for 10 minutes.
7. Add the sauce over the bok choy and serve hot.

Spice Popcorn

Prep Time: 10 minutes, Cook Time: 10 minutes, Serves: 4

INGREDIENTS:
SPICE BLEND:
6 green cardamom pods, seeds removed and husks discarded
4 whole cloves
4 black peppercorns
1 whole star anise, seeds removed and husks discarded
1 tsp. ground ginger
1 tsp. ground cinnamon
1 tsp. coriander seeds
1 tsp. fennel seeds
½ tsp. ground turmeric
⅛ tsp. ground cayenne pepper
POPCORN:
½ cup popcorn kernels
2 tbsps. vegetable oil
Kosher salt

DIRECTIONS:
MAKE THE SPICE BLEND:
1. Combine the star anise seeds, cardamom seeds, cloves, peppercorns, coriander seeds and fennel seeds in a small sauté pan or skillet. Heat the skillet over medium heat and slowly shake and swirl the spices around the pan. Toast the spices for about 5 to 6 minutes, or until you can smell the spices and they start to pop.
2. Take the pan from the heat and transfer the spices to a mortar and pestle or spice grinder. Cool the spices for about 2 minutes before grinding. Carefully grind the spices to a fine powder and take to a small bowl.
3. Place the ground cinnamon, turmeric, ginger and cayenne pepper and stir to combine well. Keep aside.
MAKE THE POPCORN:
4. Heat a wok over high heat until it just begins to smoke. Add the vegetable oil and ghee and swirl to coat the wok well. Place 2 popcorn kernels to the wok and cover. Once they pop, put the rest of the kernels and cover. Shake frequently until the popping stops and turn off the heat.
5. Take the popcorn to a large paper bag. Season with 2 generous pinches of kosher salt and 1½ tbsps. of the spice blend. Gently fold the bag closed and shake! Pour into a large bowl and enjoy hot.

Honey Shrimp with Walnut

Prep Time: 35 minutes, Cook Time: 5 minutes, Serves: 4 to 6

INGREDIENTS:
SHRIMP MARINADE:
1 pound (454 g) shrimp, peeled and deveined
2 tsps. baking soda
Pinch salt
Pinch ground white pepper
WALNUTS:
½ cup walnuts
¼ cup sugar
¼ cup water
SAUCE:
1½ tbsps. mayonnaise
1 tsp. sweetened condensed milk
1 tsp. honey
½ tsp. lemon juice
STIR-FRY:
2 tbsps. peanut oil
3 tsps. cornstarch

DIRECTIONS:
1. Add the baking soda over the shrimp and slowly massage it into the shrimp. Let the shrimp rest in the refrigerator for about 30 minutes, then thoroughly wash off the baking soda. Blot any excess water from the shrimp with a paper towel. Season with the salt and pepper.
2. While the shrimp is marinating in the cornstarch, add the sugar and water into a wok over medium-high heat. Stir until the syrup looks a light caramel color. Pour in the walnuts, stirring to coat evenly. After 1 minute, place the walnuts onto parchment paper or aluminum foil and spread them evenly with a wok spatula. Allow them to cool.
3. Prepare the sauce by combining the mayonnaise, honey, condensed milk and lemon juice in a small bowl. Keep it aside.
4. In a wok, heat the peanut oil over medium-high heat.
5. Dredge the shrimp in the cornstarch, shake off the excess, and put them in the wok in a single layer. Cook for 1 minute on one side, then stir-fry until they are completely cooked and take them to a bowl.
6. Place the candied walnuts to the shrimp, followed by the sauce, stirring to coat evenly.
7. Serve hot.

Honey-Garlic Chicken and Broccoli

Prep Time: 15 minutes, Cook Time: 6 minutes, Serves: 4

INGREDIENTS:
1 pound (454 g) boneless chicken thighs, cut into 1-inch pieces
1 cup broccoli florets, cut into bite-size pieces
1 medium carrot, roll-cut into ½-inch pieces
1 medium onion, cut into 1-inch pieces
1 red bell pepper, cut into 1-inch pieces
4 scallions, cut into 1-inch pieces
3 garlic cloves, crushed and chopped
2 tbsps. cooking oil
2 tbsps. soy sauce
2 tbsps. honey
1 tbsp. cornstarch
1 tbsp. ginger, crushed and chopped

DIRECTIONS:
1. Whisk together the soy sauce, honey, and cornstarch in a small bowl. Keep aside.
2. In a wok, heat the cooking oil over high heat until it shimmers.
3. Add the garlic, ginger, carrot and chicken and stir-fry for about 1 minute.
4. Place the onion and stir-fry for about 1 minute.
5. Put the broccoli and bell pepper and stir-fry for about 1 minute.
6. Pour soy sauce mixture to the wok and stir until a glaze is formed.
7. Sprinkle with the scallions and serve warm.

Chicken and Black Beans Tacos

Prep Time: 20 minutes, Cook Time: 45 minutes, Serves: 12

INGREDIENTS:
1 pound (454 g) boneless chicken, cut into ¾-inch cubes
1 (16-ounce / 454-g) package yellow rice
1 (16-ounce / 454-g) can black beans, rinsed and drained
12 corn tortillas
1½ cups shredded Mexican cheese blend
4 cups water
1 (4-ounce / 113-g) can sliced olives
1 (1-ounce / 28-g) package chicken taco seasoning mix
1 jalapeño pepper, seeded and minced
5 tbsps. olive oil, divided (optional)
1 tbsp. vegetable shortening

DIRECTIONS:
1. In a pan over high heat, add the water and bring to a boil.
2. Place the rice and ¼ cup of the olive oil and bring to a boil.
3. Turn the heat to medium-low and simmer, covered for 20 to 25 minutes.
4. In a wok over medium heat, heat 1 tbsp. of the olive oil and stir fry the chicken and taco seasoning mix for 5 to 10 minutes.
5. Stir in the rice, black beans, olives, Mexican cheese blend and jalapeño pepper and cook for 5 minutes.
6. In another wok on medium-high heat, warm each tortillas for 1 to 2 minutes.
7. Fill each tortilla with about ½ cup of the chicken mixture, gently folding tortilla over filling.
8. In a wok on medium heat, heat the shortening and fry the filled tortillas for 2 to 3 minutes per side. Serve warm.

Quick Drunken Shrimp

Prep Time: 30 minutes, Cook Time: 10 minutes, Serves: 4

INGREDIENTS:
1 pound (454 g) jumbo shrimp, peeled and deveined, tails left on
2 cups Shaoxing rice wine
4 peeled fresh ginger slices, each about the size of a quarter
2 tbsps. vegetable oil
2 tbsps. dried goji berries (optional)
2 tsps. sugar
2 tsps. cornstarch
Kosher salt

DIRECTIONS:
1. Stir together the rice wine, ginger, goji berries (if using) and sugar in a wide mixing bowl, until the sugar is dissolved. Place the shrimp and cover. Marinate in the refrigerator for about 20 to 30 minutes.
2. Pour the shrimp and marinade into a colander set over a bowl. Reserve ½ cup of the marinade and discard the rest.
3. Heat a wok over high heat until a drop of water sizzles and evaporates on contact. Add the oil and swirl to coat the base of the wok well. Season the oil with a small pinch of salt, and swirl slowly.
4. Place the shrimp and vigorously stir-fry, putting a pinch of salt as you flip and toss the shrimp around in the wok. Keep moving the shrimp around for 3 minutes, until they just become pink.
5. Stir the cornstarch into the reserved marinade and pour it over the shrimp. Toss the shrimp and coat with the marinade evenly. It will thicken into a glossy sauce as it begins to boil, for another 5 minutes more.
6. Take the shrimp and goji berries to a platter, remove and discard the ginger. Serve hot.

Hoisin Sesame Tofu

Prep Time: 5 minutes, Cook Time: 5 minutes, Serves: 2 to 4

INGREDIENTS:
SAUCE:
2 tsps. sesame oil
2 tbsps. hoisin sauce
1 tbsp. honey
1 tsp. soy sauce
STIR-FRY:
1 block firm tofu, cut into 1- to 1½-inch cubes
1 scallion, chopped
2 tbsps. peanut oil
1 tsp. toasted sesame seeds

DIRECTIONS:
1. Make the sauce by combining the hoisin sauce, honey, sesame oil and soy sauce in a small bowl. Keep aside.
2. In a wok, heat the peanut oil over medium-high heat.
3. Gently drop the tofu cubes into the wok, and let the bottom side cook for 20 seconds before slowly flipping them over.
4. Once the tofu is cooked on all sides, top with the sauce, slowly stirring to coat the tofu cubes.
5. Take the tofu to a serving plate. Sprinkle with the sesame seeds and chopped scallion. Serve warm.

Five-Spice Pork Meatballs

Prep Time: 10 minutes, Cook Time: 10 minutes, Makes: 20 meatballs

INGREDIENTS:
1 pound (454 g) ground pork
3 garlic cloves, minced
3 tbsps. peanut oil
1 tbsp. cornstarch
2 tsps. brown sugar
2 tsps. soy sauce
1 tsp. five-spice powder
1 tsp. minced ginger
2 pinches ground white pepper

DIRECTIONS:
1. Combine the pork, cornstarch, ginger, garlic, brown sugar, soy sauce, five-spice powder and pepper in a large bowl, and mix well.
2. Roll 1 heaping tbsp. of pork mixture into a ball and continue until all the pork mixture is used.
3. In a wok, heat the peanut oil over medium heat. Spread the oil to coat enough of the wok surface with a wok spatula to fry 10 meatballs at a time.
4. Arrange the meatballs into the wok in batches. Cook without moving for 2 minutes, or until the bottoms are cooked through. With the spatula, carefully rotate the meatballs to cook on the other sides.
5. Keep rotating the meatballs slowly until cooked through. Serve warm.

Steamed Cabbage and Carrot Dumplings

Prep Time: 20 minutes, Cook Time: 10 minutes, Makes: 15 to 20 dumplings

INGREDIENTS:
DUMPLINGS:
15 to 20 round wonton wrappers
4 cups shredded cabbage
1 carrot, shredded
5 to 8 garlic chives, cut into 1-inch pieces
2 scallions, chopped
1-inch piece of ginger, peeled and minced
1 tbsp. water
2 tsps. olive oil
2 tsps. sesame oil, plus 2 tsps. for brushing
Salt
Pepper
DIPPING SAUCE:
1-inch piece of ginger, peeled and finely minced
2 tsps. sesame oil
2 tbsps. soy sauce
2 tsps. rice vinegar
1 tsp. chili oil

DIRECTIONS:
1. In a wok, heat the olive oil over medium heat.
2. Place the cabbage, carrot, garlic chives, scallions and ginger to the wok. Stir-fry for 1 minute.
3. Pour the water to help steam the vegetables. Stir-fry until most of the water has evaporated. Add 2 tsps. of sesame oil over the vegetables. Season with salt and pepper to taste, and toss well. Turn off the heat and keep it aside to cool.
4. Put about 1 tsp. of vegetable mixture in the middle of a wonton wrapper.
5. Dampen the edges of the wonton wrapper with a little water, gently fold the wrapper in half so that it forms a triangle, and slowly press down to seal the edges.
6. Brush the dumplings with a light coating of sesame oil.
7. Gently line a bamboo steamer with parchment paper liners. Place the dumplings on top and steam for about 8 minutes, or until the wonton wrappers turn slightly translucent.
8. While the dumplings are steaming, make the dipping sauce. In a small bowl, combine the soy sauce, sesame oil, chili oil, rice vinegar and ginger.
9. Serve the dumplings with the dipping sauce.

Appendix 1: Measurement Conversion Chart

Volume Equivalents (Dry)

US STANDARD	METRIC (APPROXIMATE)
1/8 teaspoon	0.5 mL
1/4 teaspoon	1 mL
1/2 teaspoon	2 mL
3/4 teaspoon	4 mL
1 teaspoon	5 mL
1 tablespoon	15 mL
1/4 cup	59 mL
1/2 cup	118 mL
3/4 cup	177 mL
1 cup	235 mL
2 cups	475 mL
3 cups	700 mL
4 cups	1 L

Temperatures Equivalents

FAHRENHEIT (F)	CELSIUS(C) (APPROXIMATE)
225 °F	107 °C
250 °F	120 °C
275 °F	135 °C
300 °F	150 °C
325 °F	160 °C
350 °F	180 °C
375 °F	190 °C
400 °F	205 °C
425 °F	220 °C
450 °F	235 °C
475 °F	245 °C
500 °F	260 °C

Volume Equivalents (Liquid)

US STANDARD	US STANDARD (OUNCES)	METRIC (APPROXIMATE)
2 tablespoons	1 fl.oz.	30 mL
1/4 cup	2 fl.oz.	60 mL
1/2 cup	4 fl.oz.	120 mL
1 cup	8 fl.oz.	240 mL
1 1/2 cup	12 fl.oz.	355 mL
2 cups or 1 pint	16 fl.oz.	475 mL
4 cups or 1 quart	32 fl.oz.	1 L
1 gallon	128 fl.oz.	4 L

Weight Equivalents

US STANDARD	METRIC (APPROXIMATE)
1 ounce	28 g
2 ounces	57 g
5 ounces	142 g
10 ounces	284 g
15 ounces	425 g
16 ounces (1 pound)	455 g
1.5 pounds	680 g
2 pounds	907 g

Appendix 2: Recipes Index

A

Asparagus
Chicken with Asparagus   55

B

Bacon
Japanese Fried Rice with Bacon   21
Kimchi Fried Rice with Mushroom   25

Banana
Vanilla Banana Bites   77

Bean Sprout
Stir-Fried Bean Sprouts with Carrot   8
Fried Vermicelli Noodles with Mushrooms   27
Crab Egg Foo Young Patties   77

Beef
South American Pasta and Beef Salad   45
Mexican Mac n Cheese with Beef   64
Beef Empanadas   65
Beef Ramen with Pepperoni Stir-Fry   71
Corned Beef   73
Beef with Cranberry Sauce   73

Beef Brisket
Easy Quesadillas   67

Beef Flank Steak
Rice Noodles with Beef and Broccoli   28
Tasty Beef Chow Fun   30
Beef and Butternut Squash Stir Fry   66
Mongolian Beef Steak   69
Beef Steak and Bell Peppers Stir-Fry   69

Beef Round Steak
Sweet and Sour Beef Stir Fry   73

Beef Sirloin Tip
Beef Lo Mein with Bean Sprouts   31

Beef Steak
Hot and Sour Beef and Carrot Soup   50

Beef Tenderloin
Beef Tenderloin with Shiitake Mushrooms   68
Beef with Honey and Oyster Sauce   69
Sichuan Beef with Carrot   71

Beef Top Round Steak
Sesame Carrots and Steak Stir Fry   72

Black Bean
Mexican Wok Black Beans and Zucchinis   18
Healthy Black Beans with Apples   19
Peppery Bean and Spinach Salad   43

Bok Choy
Bok Choy with Ginger   8
Mediterranean Baby Bok Choy   9
Chinese North Bok Choy   10
Tianjin Stir Fry Vegetables   10
Stir-Fried Bok Choy   11
Suzhou Five Spice Bok Choy with Cashews   11
Ningbo Stir Fry Vegetables   11
Vegetarian Bok Choy   13
Appetizer Bok Choy   78

Broccoli
Luncheon Brussels Sprouts with Broccoli   11
Broccoli with Braised Mushrooms   13

Brussels Sprouts
Honey Brussels Sprouts   12
Brussels Sprouts with Pistachios   13
Maple Brussels Sprouts Stir Fry   14

C

Cabbage
Basic Stir-Fried Cabbage   12
Steamed Cabbage and Carrot Dumplings   80

Cannellini Bean
Savory Bean and Tomato Salad   43
Butternut Squash and Bean Salad   44

Carrot
Cold Scallion Noodles   27

Cashews
Basmati Rice with Cashews   23

Cauliflower
Asian Teriyaki Cauliflower and Kale   9

Chicken
Chicken and Vegetables Stir-Fry Soup   51
West African Chicken and Tomato Rice   58
Garlic Kimchi Chicken and Cabbage   61
Chicken and Vegetables with Hoisin Sauce   61
Chicken and Black Beans Tacos   79

Chicken Breast
Mexican Stir Fry Chicken and Black Beans   53
Sesame Honey Chicken   54
Chicken with Chipotle Gravy   54

Cheesy Chipotle Chicken Sandwich 54
Classic General Tso's Chicken 55
Ginger Chicken in Peanut Oil 56
Chicken with Bamboo Shoots and Mushrooms 58
Chicken Stir Fry with Peanut Butter 59
Garlic Chicken with Cashew Nuts 60
Yellow Curry Chicken with Cauliflower 60
Curry Chicken, Carrot and Zucchini 60
Chicken with Walnuts 61
Orange Chicken with Sesame Seeds 62

Chicken Drumstick
Sesame Oil Ginger Chicken 59

Chicken Leg
Chicken and Walnut Pomegranate Stew 51

Chicken Tender
East-Indian Chicken with Apricot Preserves 53

Chicken Thigh
Chicken Chow Mein with Bok Choy 32
Canton Pancit 32
Pad Thai Chicken and Rice Noodles 53
Honey Chicken 55
Coconut Chicken Thigh 56
Orange Chicken and Sugar Snap 56
Stir-Fried Chicken and Mushroom 57
Cilantro-Lime Chicken and Pineapple 57
Sweet and Sour Pineapple and Chicken 57
Lemongrass Chicken and Bok Choy 58
Kadai Chicken with Yogurt 59
Cambodian Chicken Basil Pesto 61
Honey-Garlic Chicken and Broccoli 79

Chinese Broccoli
Garlic Broccoli 12

Chinese Sausage
Steamed Rice with Chinese Sausage and Bok Choy 22
Chinese Sausage Fried Rice with Peas 24

Clam
Asian Stir-Fried Chili Clams 36

Cod
Fried Chips and Cod Fish 34
Japanese Miso Cod with Tea Rice 39

Crab
Simple Ginger and Scallion Crab 38

Crab Leg
Garlic King Crab with Hoisin Sauce 41

E

Ear Corn
Simple Cambodia Corn 9

Edamame
Roasted Red Pepper and Edamame Salad 45

Eggplant
Garlic Eggplant 8

G

Garbanzo Bean
Curry Garbanzo with Tomato 19

Garlic
Simple Sinangag 25
Egg Noodles with Scallions 31

Grape Tomato
Easy Tomato Egg Stir-Fry 77

Green Bean
Authentic Beans Caprese 16
Seared Tofu with Green Beans and Coconut Sauce 16
Saucy Green Beans Skillet 17
Green Bean with Chicken Thighs 17
Venetian Garlic Beans 18
Noodles with Green Beans and Cabbage 18
Caramelized Balsamic Bean with Onion 18
Tuna and Beans Salad 44

H

Halibut
French Inspired Halibut 40

L

Lamb
Lamb with Pear and Prunes 68

Lamb Leg
Stir-Fried Ginger Lamb 66
Lamb Leg with Ginger and Leeks 67
Sichuan Cumin-Spiced Lamb 67

Lobster
Seafood Salad 43

M

Mint
Indian Fried Rice with Onion 21

Mushroom
Couscous Ghardaïa with Mushroom 22
Chinese Mushroom and Carrot Soup 48

Mussel

Ginger Mussels in Black Bean Sauce 34
Sichuan Mussels and Shrimp 40
Mussels with Tomato Sauce 41

N

Nut
Mixed Nut Pilaf with Herbes 23

O

Onion
Alexandria Nutty Rice Casserole 22

Orange Lentil
Ginger Orange Lentil Stew 16

P

Pea
Vegetable Egg Fried Rice 25
Egg Foo Yong with Peas 76

Peanut
Simple Sweet Peanut Soup 47

Pork
Hakka Noodles with Pork and Cabbage 29
Pork and Shrimp Wonton Soup 47
Hot and Sour Noodle with Pork Soup 49
Healthy Pork Congee 49
Healthy Pork and Egg Drop Soup 50
Pork with Bok Choy and Carrot 64
Steamed Egg with Ground Pork 70
Five-Spice Pork Meatballs 80

Pork Belly
Twice-Cooked Pork Belly with Black Bean Sauce 71

Pork Loin
Hoisin Pork and Snow Peas Stir-Fry 64

Pork Rib
Quick Peking-Style Pork Ribs 65
Stir-Fried Pork Ribs with Black Bean Sauce 65

Pork Shoulder
Sichuan Twice-Cooked Pork with Leek 70

Pork Sparerib
Pork Ribs with Black Bean Sauce 68

Pork Tenderloin
Honey Pork 70
Pork and Mushroom Lettuce Wraps 75

Potato
Curry Veggie Caribbean Style 9

R

Red Grape
Grape Chutney with Herbes 8

Romaine Lettuce
Healthy Baby Romaine with Goji Berries 13

S

Salmon
Teriyaki Salmon with Sugar Snap 38
Salmon and Vegetables with Oyster Sauce 41

Sausage
Italian Sausage Pot Pie 66
Andouille and Basmati Rice 72

Scallion
Sesame Noodles with Peanut Butter 30

Scallop
Bay Scallops with Snow Peas 37

Sea Scallop
Sweet Vietnamese Scallops and Cucumbers 36

Shrimp
Shrimp Fried Rice with Peas 23
Fried Rice with Shrimp and Egg 24
Singapore Noodles with Shrimp 28
Chinese Birthday Noodles with Shrimp 29
Seafood Lo Mein with Pork 30
Curried Shrimp with Basmati 34
Shrimp and Pork with Lobster Sauce 35
Spicy Shrimp with Pineapple and Papaya 36
Quick Shrimp with Lobster Sauce 37
Stir-Fry Shrimp and Broccoli 39
Easy Salt and Pepper Shrimp 40
Sizzling Rice and Shrimp Soup 49
Hot-Sour Seafood and Vegetables Soup 50
Shrimp and Water Chestnuts Dumplings 75
Shrimp with Roasted Peanuts 76
Honey Shrimp with Walnut 78
Quick Drunken Shrimp 79

Skirt Steak
Orange Sesame Beef 72

Snow Pea
Asian Wok Veggies with Peanut Butter Sauce 10

Spam
Spam Pineapple Fried Rice 21

Spinach

84   Appendix

Tasty Vegetarian Tanzanian Skillet 11
Stir-Fried Garlic Spinach 12

Squid
Korean Spicy Stir-Fry Squid 39
Malaysian Chili Squid and Celery 40

String Bean
Quinoa Fried Rice with Beans 19

Strip Steak
Steak with Arugula Salad 45

Sugar Snap
Honey Chow Mein with Vegetable 27

T

Tilapia
Light Seafood Congee 37

Tofu
Asian Wok Sticky Tofu and Veggies 10
Stir-Fried Bok Choy, Egg and Tofu Soup 47
Hoisin Sesame Tofu 80

Tomato
Simple Stir-Fried Tomato and Eggs 14
Indonesian Tomato Egg Fried Rice 23
Asian Spicy Pasta with Tomatoes 29
Simple Myriam's Salad 43
Tomato and Egg Drop Soup 48

Trout
Fried Rice with Smoked Trout 24

Turkey
Turkey and Bean Salad 44

W

White Fish
Pan-Fried White Fish with Soy Sauce 35
Thai White Fish and Vegetables 35
Chinese Steamed Fish 38

Whole Chicken
Chinese Chicken Stock 48
Chicken and Bacon Rice 59
Malay Whole Chicken Curry 60
Japanese Cumin Chicken Stir Fry 76

Y

Yellow Split Pea
Asian Yellow Peas with Spinach 17

Z

Zucchini
Teriyaki Vegan Combo 12

Dear Readers,
We are glad that you purchased this book, your opinion is very important to us. If you have any comments and suggestions on this cookbook, we sincerely invite you to send us an email for feedback.
With your participation, we will grow faster and better.
After receiving your email, we will upgrade the product according to your needs and give you an e-book of 50 recipes as a gift.
We are committed to continuous growth and progress, providing readers with cookbooks that help create a better kitchen life and a healthy body.
I wish you happy every day.

Company contact email: Healthrecipegroup@outlook.com

Printed in Great Britain
by Amazon